WikiNLP: Advancing Natural Language Processing for Wikipedia

Vienna, Austria
1 August 2025

ISBN: 979-8-3313-2421-6

Printed from e-media with permission by:

Curran Associates, Inc.
57 Morehouse Lane
Red Hook, NY 12571

Some format issues inherent in the e-media version may also appear in this print version.

Association for Computational Linguistics
209 N. Eighth Street
Stroudsburg, Pennsylvania 18360

Phone: 1-570-476-8006
Fax: 1-570-476-0860

acl@aclweb.org

Additional copies of this publication are available from:

Curran Associates, Inc.
57 Morehouse Lane
Red Hook, NY 12571 USA
Phone: 845-758-0400
Fax: 845-758-2633
Email: curran@proceedings.com
Web: www.proceedings.com

WikiNLP 2025

WikiNLP: Advancing Natural Language Processing for Wikipedia

Proceedings of the Workshop

August 1, 2025

Program Committee

Program Chairs

Akhil Arora, Aarhus University
Isaac Johnson, Wikimedia
Lucie-Aimée Kaffee, Hugging Face
Tzu-Sheng Kuo, Carnegie Mellon University
Tiziano Piccardi, Stanford University
Indira Sen, Universität Mannheim

Reviewers

Neelima Agarwal, Pablo Aragón, Hiba Arnaout, Wenceslao Arroyo-Machado

Hsuvas Borkakoty, Hannah Brueckner

Kaylea Champion

Djellel Difallah

Patrick Gildersleve, Dipanwita Guhathakurta, Lavanya Gupta

Steve Jankowski, Srihari Jayakumar, Deeptanshu Jha

Gaurav Kumar

Isabelle Langrock

Finn Årup Nielsen

Tiziano Piccardi, Karthik Sriranga Puthraya

Marija Sakota, Nicole Schwitter, Indira Sen, Andreas Spitz

Nathan TeBlunthuis, Carla Toro, Harold Triedman, Mykola Trokhymovych

Thejas Venkatesh

Jheng-Hong Yang, Jisung Yoon

Dale Zhou, Kai Zhu

Table of Contents

Wikivecs: A Fully Reproducible Vectorization of Multilingual Wikipedia

Brandon Duderstadt
Nomic AI
brandon@nomic.ai

Abstract

Dense vector representations have become foundational to modern natural language processing (NLP), powering diverse workflows from semantic search and retrieval augmented generation to content comparison across languages. Although Wikipedia is one of the most comprehensive and widely used datasets in modern NLP research, it lacks a fully reproducible and permissively licensed dense vectorization. In this paper, we present Wikivecs, a fully reproducible, permissively licensed dataset containing dense vector embeddings for every article in Multilingual Wikipedia. Our pipeline leverages a fully reproducible and permissively licensed multilingual text encoder to embed Wikipedia articles into a unified vector space, making it easy to compare and analyze content across languages. Alongside these vectors, we release a two-dimensional data map derived from the vectors, enabling visualization and exploration of Multilingual Wikipedia's content landscape. We demonstrate the utility of our dataset by identifying several content gaps between English and Russian Wikipedia.

1 Introduction

Dense vector representations have become foundational to modern natural language processing (NLP), powering diverse workflows from semantic search to retrieval augmented generation. As multilingual models have matured, these vectors have become particularly useful for bridging linguistic and cultural gaps, offering a shared representational space where texts from different languages can be meaningfully compared.

Simultaneously, Wikipedia has become one of the most important datasets in modern NLP research. Despite its importance, there exists no openly licensed, fully reproducible resource that provides dense vectors for the entirety of Multilingual Wikipedia. This gap limits the accessibility and transparency of multilingual Wikipedia research and hinders efforts to conduct scalable, comparative content analysis across languages.

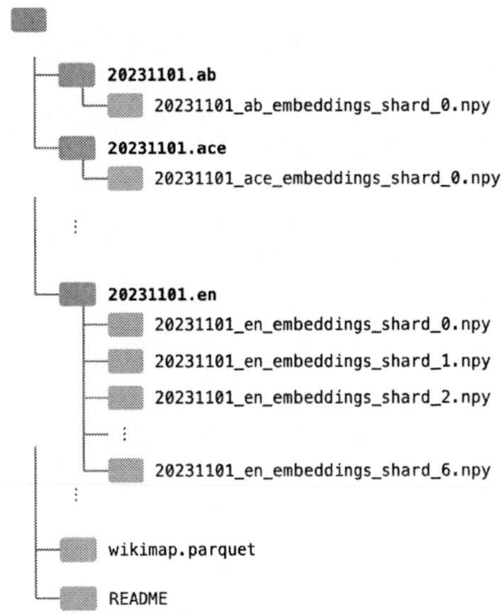

Figure 1: The directory structure of the Wikivecs dataset. Each folder corresponds to a language split and contains one or more sharded numpy arrays. When concatenated in ascending shard index order, these arrays correspond embeddings of the rows in the 2023-11-01 Wikidump dataset. For example, 20231101_en_embeddings_shard_0.npy contains embeddings for rows 0-999,999 of the Wikidump file 20231101.en, 20231101_en_embeddings_shard_1.npy contains embeddings for rows 1,000,0000-1,999,999 of the Wikidump file 20231101.en, etc... Also included in the dataset is wikimap.parquet, a file which contains 2d positions for every article in the Wikidump, enabling subsequent visualization.

In this work, we introduce Wikivecs, a fully reproducible and permissively licensed dataset of dense vector embeddings for every article in Multiulingual Wikipedia. Using a state-of-the-art multilingual encoder, Wikivecs captures the semantic content of articles in a vector space that can

Proceedings of the 2nd Workshop on Advancing Natural Language Processing for Wikipedia (WikiNLP 2025), pages 1–9
August 1, 2025 ©2025 Association for Computational Linguistics

be compared meaningfully across languages. We also leverage recent research in scalable dimensionality reduction to construct a 2 dimensional map of the entirety of Multilingual Wikipedia. We demonstrate how these resources can be used to surface topics that lack cross-lingual coverage in Wikipedia, highlighting several content gaps between English and Russian Wikipedia.

2 Background

Early methods for computational text comparison relied on normalized word count statistics (Spärck Jones, 1972) The field of text representation shifted to a much more connectionist paradigm in 2013 with the publication of Word2Vec (Mikolov et al., 2013), which used a shallow neural network to learn a vector representation for each token in a sentence based on its context.

BERT (Devlin et al., 2019) utilized the transformer (Vaswani et al., 2023) architecture to train a deep neural network to produce contextualized vector representations of tokens in an input text. BERT could also be used to compare texts by running it in a cross-encoder configuration. In the cross-encoder configuration, two input texts were fed to the BERT model together to produce a document similarity score.

Computing the pairwise similarity of all texts in a large corpus is computationally burdensome, making it difficult to utilize BERT for document comparison in large corpora. To remedy this, Reimers and Gurevych introduced SBERT (Reimers and Gurevych, 2019), which utilized a bi-encoder architecture and a triplet training procedure to map sentences to dense vectors endowed with a semantic similarity structure. This enabled document similarity to be computed efficiently by measuring the angle between documents' dense vector representations.

The efficiency of this bi-encoder approach has led it to become the dominant technique for large scale text representation and comparison. As a result, a plethora of text bi-encoders have been subsequently developed and released. (Wang et al., 2024; Xiao et al., 2024; Günther et al., 2024; Nussbaum et al., 2024; Li et al., 2023; Chen et al., 2024).

Unfortunately, the almost all state-of-the-art bi-encoders are not suitable for open science and open knowledge use, since large parts of their training recipe (e.g. training data, training code, weights, etc...) remain proprietary or are restrictively licensed. In contrast, the recently released Nomic-Embed-Text-v2 (Nussbaum and Duderstadt, 2025) is the first state-of-the-art multilingual bi-encoder to release all the elements of its training recipe under a permissive Apache 2.0 license, making it an ideal candidate for open science and open knowledge work.

wikimap.parquet (61,614,907 rows)

Column	Type	Description
x	float	X-coordinate for visualization
y	float	Y-coordinate for visualization
title	string	Wikipedia article title
subset	string	Language subset identifier
url	string	Wikipedia article URL
wid	integer	Wikipedia article ID

Figure 2: The schema of wikimap.parquet

Table 1: NOMAD Projection Hyperparameters

Hyperparameter	**Value**
n noise	10,000
n neighbors	64
n cells	128
epochs	600
momentum	0.0
lr scale	0.1
learning rate decay start time	0.1
late exaggeration time	0.7
late exaggeration scale	1.5
batch size	70,000
cluster subset size	2,500,000
cluster chunk size	1,000

3 Dataset Description

Our dataset is an extension of the 2023-11-01 Wikidump dataset (Wikimedia), which we accessed via Hugging Face.

We produce a dense vector for each article in the Wikidump using Nomic-Embed-Text-v2, a fully open and permissively licensed multilingual text embedding model. Each article is truncated to the first 512 tokens so that it fits in the Nomic-Embed-Text-v2 context window, and no task specific prefixes are prepended to the article texts. Nomic-Embed-Text-v2 then converts each article to a 768 dimensional dense vector. These article vectors are saved in shards corresponding to each of the language splits in the Wikidump. Figure 1 details the directory structure of the resulting shards. We note that process of generating and storing these vectors

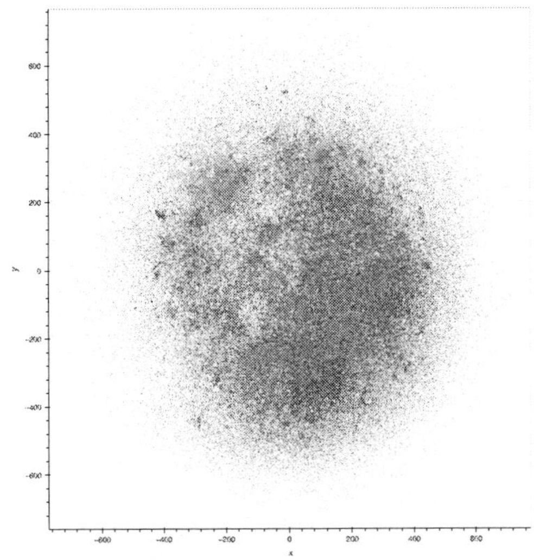

(a) A data map overlaying the English (purple) and Russian (green) Wikipedia corpora. Some areas contain dots of both colors, indicating conceptual overlap. Other areas contain dots of only one color, indicating a potential content gap.

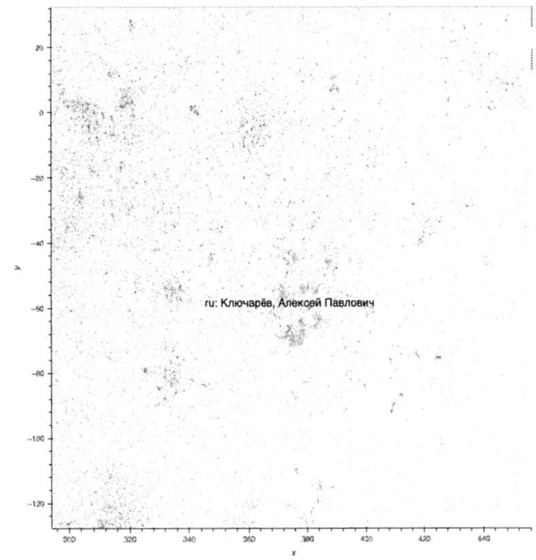

(b) A zoomed view of the English-Russian Wikipedia data map. The location of an article on Ключарёв, Алексей Павлович is indicated. Further investigation reveals article is about a Russian Nuclear Physicist, and that it has no English translation. Analysis of the surrounding cluster reveals that it is a cluster of articles about Russian scientists, most of which lack English translations.

Figure 3: Comparison of English and Russian Wikipedia content coverage

is nontrivial, requiring several H100 days of compute, and resulting in approximately a terabyte of data.

Nomic-Embed-Text-v2 achieves state-of-the-art performance on the MIRACL benchmark (Zhang et al., 2022), as well as strong performance on the bitext mining task of the MMTEB benchmark (Enevoldsen et al., 2025). As a result, we can reasonably expect the vectors it produces to map semantically similar content in different languages to similar locations in vector space. This property enables downstream cross-lingual analysis using the produced vectors.

Once all the articles are vectorized, we apply NOMAD Projection (Duderstadt et al., 2025), a scalable nonlinear dimensionality reduction algorithm, to project them into a 2d space for subsequent visualization and inference. We run NOMAD Projection with the hyperparameters outlined in Table 1. The output of NOMAD Projection is used to generate wikimap.parquet, whose schema is detailed in Figure 2. A key benefit of the 2d Wikivecs is their size; working with the 2d vectors enables meaningful corpus analysis to be performed on a standard laptop, greatly increasing the accessibility of our dataset.

4 Access and Reproduction

All of the choices in our vectorization pipeline were made with accessibility and reproducibility in mind. Nomic-Embed-Text-v2 releases its training data, code, and weights under a permissive license, meaning the Wikivectors themselves have fully open provenance. Further, all code for generating the vectors, as well as the subsequent visualizations, is open sourced and permissively licensed. Finally, the 2d vectorization alleviates the large computational burden of working with the 768 dimensional vectors, enabling meaningful corpus analysis to be performed on a standard laptop.

The final dataset can be accessed at https://huggingface.co/datasets/nomic-ai/nomic-embed-v2-wikivecs, and the code for reproducing the dataset can be accessed at https://github.com/nomic-ai/wikivecs.

5 Example Application: Cross Lingual Content Gap Analysis

As an example of the utility of our dataset, we use the 2d positions derived from the Wikivecs to surface content gaps between English and Russian Wikipedia. We define a content gap as a collec-

Article Title	English	Russian
Ключарёв, Алексей Павлович	No	Yes
Глазков, Анатолий Александрович	No	Yes
Воробьёв, Леонид Евгеньевич	No	Yes
Загорец, Павел Авксентьевич	No	Yes
Харитонов, Анатолий Михайлович	No	Yes
Разборов, Александр Александрович	Yes	Yes
Рябинин, Валериан Николаевич	No	Yes
Аржаников, Николай Сергеевич	No	Yes
Золотов, Юрий Александрович (химик)	No	Yes
Левшин, Геннадий Егорович	No	Yes
Total	1	10

Table 2: Ten articles about Russian scientists from a homogeneously colored region in the interactive data exploration application. Manual investigation reveals that English Wikipedia lacks articles on almost all of these scientists, indicating a content gap.

tion of thematically related articles that exist in one language, but not another language. Our dataset enables both qualitative and quantitative surfacing of content gaps. We perform both the qualitative and quantitative analysis on a standard M2 Macbook Air with 24GB of RAM, which highlights the accessibility of the 2d vectors.

5.1 Qualitative Analysis: Interactive Data Explorer

To facilitate the qualitative discovery of content gaps between different languages on Wikipedia, we created an interactive data exploration application for the 2d positions in the Wikivecs corpus. The application plots the 2d positions of articles in two or more language splits of Wikivecs as differently colored dots in a scatter plot. The explorer enables users to pan and zoom the plot, hover their mouse over dots to reveal article titles, and click on dots to open their associated articles in a new tab. The application workflow facilitates the investigation and discovery of content gaps across Multilingual Wikipedia.

Figure 3a shows the application comparing English (purple) and Russian (green) Wikipedia. Some areas of the plot contain dots of both colors, indicating conceptual overlap. Other areas contain dots of only one color, indicating a potential content gap.

Figure 3b shows a zoomed in view of an area in the English-Russian Wikipedia data map containing a concentration of green dots. This area of the map corresponds to articles about Russian scientists on Russian Wikipedia. The location of an article on Ключарёв, Алексей Павлович is indicated by the green X. Google translate reveals that this article is about Alexey Pavlovich Klyucharyov, the head of the Nuclear Physics Department at Kharkov University from 1943-1944. We manually verify that Alexey Pavlovich Klyucharyov has no corresponding article in English Wikipedia.

We further investigate this potential content gap by manually inspecting 9 other articles that are proximal to Alexey Pavlovich Klyucharyov in the data explorer. The results of our manual inspection are presented in Table 2. Overall, we find that 9 out of the 10 Russian Wikipedia articles we selected did not have counterparts on English Wikipedia, indicating a content gap.

The discovery of this cluster of Russian scientists who have no matching articles in English Wikipedia demonstrates our dataset's utility for powering qualitative applications that surface content gaps between language splits on Wikipedia.

5.2 Quantitative Analysis: Cluster Entropy

To further investigate content gaps between English and Russian Wikipedia, we cluster the 2d positions in the English-Russian Wikipedia map, and investigate clusters with low inter-cluster language distribution entropy.

We start by training a decision tree to partition the 2d map positions into regions of low linguistic entropy. We use a held-out validation set consisting of a random sample of 20% of the English and Russian Wikivec data to determine the maximum depth hyperparameter of our decision tree, and we use a minimum leaf size of 10 to prevent small clusters from forming in our tree. The results of our hyperparameter sweep are presented in Figure

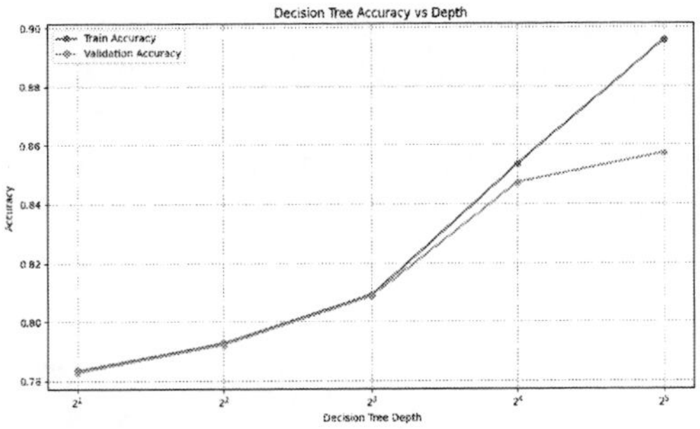

(a) The accuracy of decision tree classifiers trained to predict article languages given their 2d positions in the Wikivecs dataset. The train and validation accuracy curves deviate after a maximum tree depth of 2^4, indicating overfitting. As a result, a maximum tree depth of 2^4 is selected for the final decision tree.

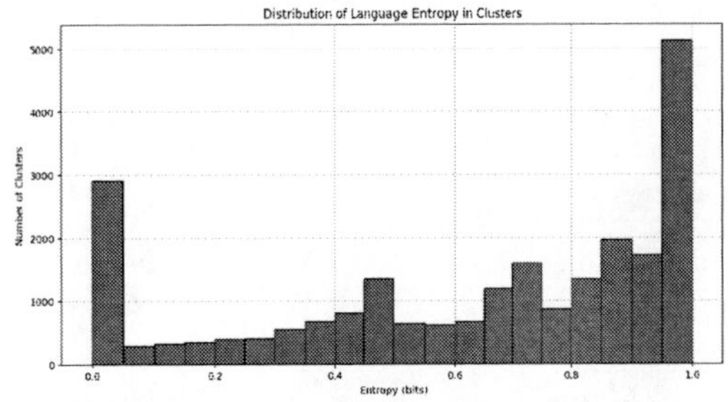

(b) A histogram of the entropy of the language distribution in clusters derived from 2d positions of English and Russian articles in the Wikivecs dataset. There are nearly 3000 clusters with 0 bits of entropy, meaning that they consist entirely of articles in a single language.

Figure 4: Decision tree classifier analysis: (a) Accuracy vs. tree depth showing overfitting beyond depth 2^4, and (b) Entropy distribution of language clusters showing many pure single-language clusters.

4a.

We train a final decision tree with a maximum depth of 2^4 and a minimum leaf size of 10 on all the 2d positions corresponding to English and Russian articles in the Wikivecs dataset. We then interpret the leaf nodes of this decision tree as clusters, and compute the entropy of the language distribution in each cluster. Clusters with a low entropy correspond to spatially localized regions in the map consisting almost entirely of articles in a single language, making them strong candidates to investigate for content gaps.

Figure 4b shows a histogram of the clusters' language distribution entropies. There are a large number of clusters with 0 bits of entropy, meaning that they consist entirely of articles in a single language.

To get a sense of whether these zero entropy clusters actually correspond to content gaps, we manually inspect 10 random articles from three random zero entropy clusters. The results of our manual inspection are presented in Tables 3, 4, and 5. We find that all three clusters contain articles with coherent themes; namely, Beetles, Bibilical Codex, and Hungarian Villages. This is a positive indication that our vectors effectively group articles according to their semantics.

In the Beetles cluster, we find that only 1 of the 10 articles has a Russian translation. Similarly, in the Hungarian Villages cluster, we find that none of the articles have Russian translations. As a result, we conclude that both of these clusters represent thematic content gaps between English and Russian Wikipedia.

In the Biblical Codex cluster, we find that 6 of the 10 articles have Russian translations. This indicates that Russian Wikipedia has coverage of some of the content in this theme. We conclude that this cluster may not represent a content gap between English and Russian Wikipedia.

Overall, the manual verification confirms that our pipeline is able to surface strong candidates for thematic content gaps between English and Russian Wikipedia.

Article Title	English	Russian
Amara exarata	Yes	No
Amara fusca	Yes	No
Amara familiaris	Yes	No
Amara alpina	Yes	Yes
Amara praetermissa	Yes	No
Amara confusa	Yes	No
Amara quenseli	Yes	No
Amara pomona	Yes	No
Amara latior	Yes	No
Amara rubrica	Yes	No
Total	10	1

Table 3: Cluster: 34853 - Beetles

6 Conclusion

In this paper we introduced Wikivecs, the first open source, fully reproducible, and permissively licensed dense vectorization of Multilingual Wikipedia. We generate a 768 dimensional dense vector representation of each article on Multilingual Wikipedia using a fully reproducible and per-

Article Title	English	Russian
Hencse	Yes	No
Kálmáncsa	Yes	No
Fonyód District	Yes	No
Nagyberény	Yes	No
Szentbalázs	Yes	No
Gamás	Yes	No
Öreglak	Yes	No
Bélavár	Yes	No
Marcali	Yes	No
Nagykorpád	Yes	No
Total	10	0

Table 4: Cluster: 29172 - Hungarian Villages

Article Title	English	Russian
Codex Bezae	Yes	Yes
Codex Vaticanus 2061	Yes	Yes
Codex Marchalianus	Yes	Yes
Codex Speculum	Yes	No
Codex Brixianus	Yes	No
Codex Toletanus	Yes	Yes
Codex Sangallensis 1395	Yes	No
Codex Vaticanus 1829	Yes	No
Codex Agobardinus	Yes	No
Codex Boernerianus	Yes	Yes
Total	10	6

Table 5: Cluster: 40931 - Biblical Codex

missively licensed multilingual text embedder. We then perform large scale nonlinear dimensionality reduction on the 768 dimensional vectors to assign every article in Multilingual Wikipedia a position in a 2d semantic map.

As an example of the utility of our dataset, we use both qualitative and quantitative methods to surface content gaps between English and Russian Wikipedia. Qualitatively, we contribute an interactive data exploration application that enables users to visually compare the coverage of different Wikipedia language splits. We use this application to surface a content gap related to Russian scientists who lack articles in English Wikipedia. Quantitatively, we train a decision tree to surface spatially localized regions of low language entropy in the 2d semantic map. Manual investigation of a random sample of these low-entropy regions surfaces content gaps relating to beetles and Hungarian villages on Russian Wikipedia. We run both our qualitative and quantitative analysis on a standard M2 Macbook Air with 24GB of RAM, highlighting the accessibility of our dataset.

Overall, we believe that our dataset will significantly lower the barrier to performing modern NLP application development and analysis on Multilingual Wikipedia.

Limitations

There are several important limitations to consider regarding our dataset.

The Wikivecs corpus is nearly a terabyte of data resulting from several H100 days of processing time. Its scale undoubtedly affects scientists' ability to reproduce and analyze it in its entirety. We attempted to address this by contributing the much more wieldy 2d vectorization in conjuncton with the 768 dimensional vectorization, but the generalization of findings from the 2d vectors to the 768 dimensional vectors represents a limitation in and of itself.

Additionally, the quantitative and qualitative analyses we provided regarding content gaps could be expanded significantly. In particular, we were hindered by the highly manual process of verifying whether or not the clusters we surfaced indeed represented true content gaps. As a result, our evaluations were limited to one language comparison (English-Russian), and were quantified using relatively low evaluation set sample sizes. It is our hope that the release of this dataset will accelerate a much wider community effort to understand and validate content gaps across Multilingual Wikipedia.

Benefits and Risks

How does this work benefit the Wikipedia community? Our work stands to significantly benefit the Wikipedia community. Understanding and rectifying content gaps across different Wikipedia languages is an issue of central importance in the community, and our work demonstrably accelerates work in this area. More broadly, we believe that our work will enable researchers to much more easily build NLP applications and analyses with Multilingual Wikipedia.

What license are you using for your data, code, models? Are they available for community re-use? We made decisions in the interest of accessibility and reproducibility throughout the entirety of our project. We specifically selected Nomic-Embed-Text-v2 as our embedder due to its permissive Apache 2.0 license and end-to-end reproducibility. Further, we provided a 2d vectorization in addition to the much more unwieldy 768d vectorization to enable corpus analysis using much more limited compute resources. Moreover, we selected a simple and efficient quantitative content gap surfacing method specifically to enable reproducibility on a standard laptop. The entire analysis in quantitative analysis section can be run on an M2 Macbook Air with 24GB of RAM in under 10 minutes.

Finally, all artifacts, data, and models used in this paper are released to the community under a permissive MIT license.

Did you provide clear descriptions and rationale for any filtering that you applied to your data? For example, did you filter to just one language (e.g., English Wikipedia) or many? Did you filter to any specific geographies or topics? The place where we most obviously filtered our data was in our analysis, where we rather arbitrarily selected English and Russian as the languages we would investigate for content gaps. The main rationale for filtering down to two languages is because an exhaustive pairwise comparison of the content between all languages on Wikipedia is a massive undertaking, and is beyond the scope of this paper.

If there are risks from your work, do any of them apply specifically to Wikimedia editors or the projects? We do not forsee any immediate risks to Wikimedia editors or their projects as a result of our work.

Did you name any Wikimedia editors (including username) or provide information exposing an editor's identity? We neither named any Wikimedia editors nor provided information exposing any identities.

Could your research be used to infer sensitive data about individual editors? If so, please explain further. We do not believe our work meaningfully accelerates the ability of any actors to deanonymize any individual editors.

References

Jianlv Chen, Shitao Xiao, Peitian Zhang, Kun Luo, Defu Lian, and Zheng Liu. 2024. Bge m3-embedding: Multi-lingual, multi-functionality, multi-granularity text embeddings through self-knowledge distillation. *Preprint*, arXiv:2402.03216.

Jacob Devlin, Ming-Wei Chang, Kenton Lee, and Kristina Toutanova. 2019. Bert: Pre-training of deep bidirectional transformers for language understanding. *Preprint*, arXiv:1810.04805.

Brandon Duderstadt, Zach Nussbaum, and Laurens van der Maaten. 2025. Nomad projection. *Preprint*, arXiv:2505.15511.

Kenneth Enevoldsen, Isaac Chung, Imene Kerboua, Márton Kardos, Ashwin Mathur, David Stap, Jay Gala, Wissam Siblini, Dominik Krzemiński, Genta Indra Winata, Saba Sturua, Saiteja Utpala, Mathieu Ciancone, Marion Schaeffer, Gabriel Sequeira, Diganta Misra, Shreeya Dhakal, Jonathan Rystrøm, Roman Solomatin, and 67 others. 2025. Mmteb: Massive multilingual text embedding benchmark. *Preprint*, arXiv:2502.13595.

Michael Günther, Jackmin Ong, Isabelle Mohr, Alaeddine Abdessalem, Tanguy Abel, Mohammad Kalim Akram, Susana Guzman, Georgios Mastrapas, Saba Sturua, Bo Wang, Maximilian Werk, Nan Wang, and Han Xiao. 2024. Jina embeddings 2: 8192-token general-purpose text embeddings for long documents. *Preprint*, arXiv:2310.19923.

Zehan Li, Xin Zhang, Yanzhao Zhang, Dingkun Long, Pengjun Xie, and Meishan Zhang. 2023. Towards general text embeddings with multi-stage contrastive learning. *Preprint*, arXiv:2308.03281.

Tomas Mikolov, Kai Chen, Greg Corrado, and Jeffrey Dean. 2013. Efficient estimation of word representations in vector space. *Preprint*, arXiv:1301.3781.

Zach Nussbaum and Brandon Duderstadt. 2025. Training sparse mixture of experts text embedding models. *Preprint*, arXiv:2502.07972.

Zach Nussbaum, John X. Morris, Brandon Duderstadt, and Andriy Mulyar. 2024. Nomic embed: Training a reproducible long context text embedder. *Preprint*, arXiv:2402.01613.

Nils Reimers and Iryna Gurevych. 2019. Sentence-bert: Sentence embeddings using siamese bert-networks. *Preprint*, arXiv:1908.10084.

Karen Spärck Jones. 1972. A statistical interpretation of term specificity and its application in retrieval. *Journal of Documentation*, 28(1):11–21.

Ashish Vaswani, Noam Shazeer, Niki Parmar, Jakob Uszkoreit, Llion Jones, Aidan N. Gomez, Lukasz Kaiser, and Illia Polosukhin. 2023. Attention is all you need. *Preprint*, arXiv:1706.03762.

Liang Wang, Nan Yang, Xiaolong Huang, Binxing Jiao, Linjun Yang, Daxin Jiang, Rangan Majumder, and Furu Wei. 2024. Text embeddings by weakly-supervised contrastive pre-training. *Preprint*, arXiv:2212.03533.

Wikimedia. Wikimedia downloads.

Shitao Xiao, Zheng Liu, Peitian Zhang, Niklas Muennighoff, Defu Lian, and Jian-Yun Nie. 2024. C-pack: Packed resources for general chinese embeddings. *Preprint*, arXiv:2309.07597.

Xinyu Zhang, Nandan Thakur, Odunayo Ogundepo, Ehsan Kamalloo, David Alfonso-Hermelo, Xiaoguang Li, Qun Liu, Mehdi Rezagholizadeh, and Jimmy Lin. 2022. Making a miracl: Multilingual information retrieval across a continuum of languages. *Preprint*, arXiv:2210.09984.

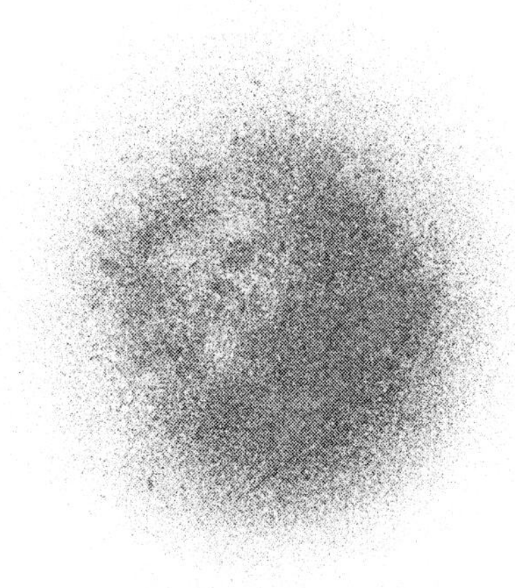

(a) English (teal) vs French (red)

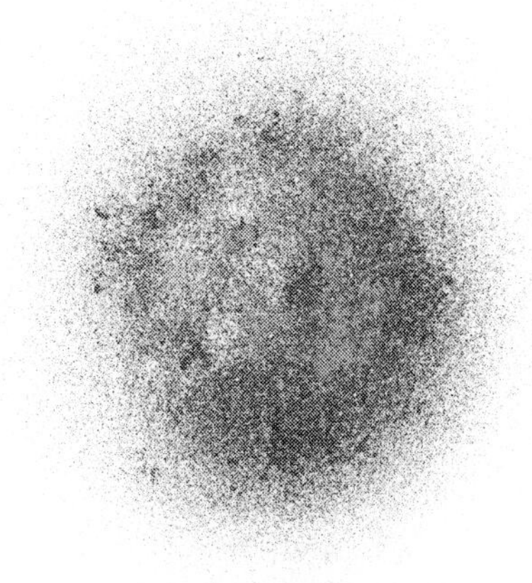

(b) English (purple) vs German (yellow)

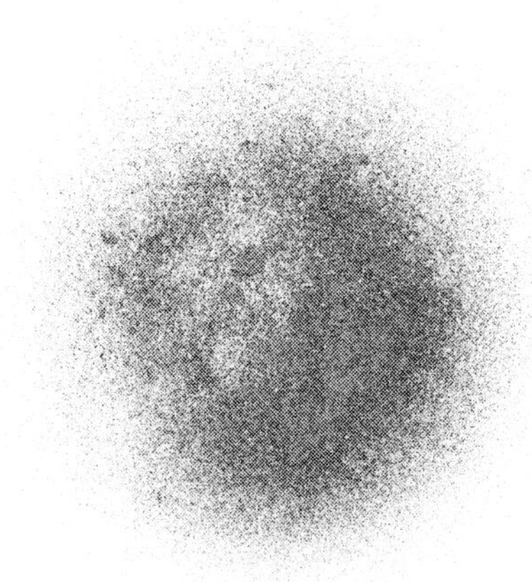

(c) English (blue) vs Spanish (orange)

(d) English (purple) vs Russian (green)

Figure 5: Additional visualizations of semantic overlap in Multilingual Wikipedia across several languages.

WETBench: A Benchmark for Detecting Task-Specific Machine-Generated Text on Wikipedia

Gerrit Quaremba[1], **Elizabeth Black**[1], **Denny Vrandečić**[2], **Elena Simperl**[1]
[1]King's College London, [2]Wikimedia Foundation
{gerrit.quaremba,elizabeth.black,elena.simperl}@kcl.ac.uk
denny@wikimedia.org

Abstract

Given Wikipedia's role as a trusted source of high-quality, reliable content, concerns are growing about the proliferation of low-quality machine-generated text (MGT) produced by large language models (LLMs) on its platform. Reliable detection of MGT is therefore essential. However, existing work primarily evaluates MGT detectors on generic generation tasks rather than on tasks more commonly performed by Wikipedia editors. This misalignment can lead to poor generalisability when applied in real-world Wikipedia contexts. We introduce **WETBench**, a multilingual, multi-generator, and *task-specific* benchmark for MGT detection. We define three editing tasks, empirically grounded in Wikipedia editors' perceived use cases for LLM-assisted editing: *Paragraph Writing*, *Summarisation*, and *Text Style Transfer*, which we implement using two new datasets across three languages. For each writing task, we evaluate three prompts, generate MGT across multiple generators using the best-performing prompt, and benchmark diverse detectors. We find that, across settings, training-based detectors achieve an average accuracy of 78%, while zero-shot detectors average 58%. These results show that detectors struggle with MGT in realistic generation scenarios and underscore the importance of evaluating such models on diverse, task-specific data to assess their reliability in editor-driven contexts.

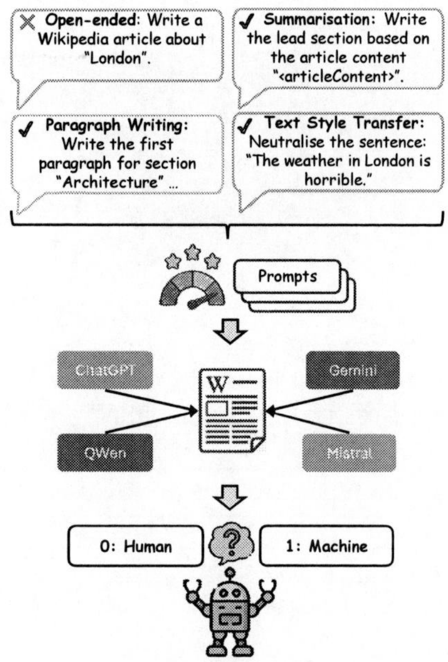

Figure 1: We define *task-specific editing scenarios* on Wikipedia, test various prompting techniques, generate LLM-written text using the best-performing prompts, and benchmark SOTA detectors on these data. This contrasts with prior work, which primarily focuses on a single, *open-ended* generation task that only partially captures the real-world editorial use of LLMs.

1 Introduction

Wikipedia serves as a vital source of high-quality, trustworthy data across artificial intelligence (AI) communities. Its scale and richness have played a foundational role in the development of large language models (LLMs) (Deckelmann, 2023; Longpre et al., 2023). However, the Wikipedia community has expressed growing concern about the increasing prevalence of machine-generated text (MGT) produced by LLMs on its platform.[1] The Wikimedia Foundation warns that the spread of low-quality, unreliable MGT in its projects could undermine its knowledge integrity.[2] Specifically, unverified MGT poses challenges such as factual fabrication (Huang et al., 2025a) and the perpetuation of biases present in training data (Gallegos et al., 2024), both of which jeop-

[1]https://en.wikipedia.org/wiki/Wikipedia:Large_language_models

[2]Wikipedia Community Call Notes 2023–24

Proceedings of the 2nd Workshop on Advancing Natural Language Processing for Wikipedia (WikiNLP 2025), pages 10–30
August 1, 2025 ©2025 Association for Computational Linguistics

ardise Wikipedia's core content policies.[3] Additionally, given Wikipedia's frequent inclusion in LLM training corpora, undetected MGT on the platform may contribute to performance degradation in future models (Shumailov et al., 2024). Consequently, distinguishing human-written from machine-generated text has become increasingly important, leading to community efforts to identify and remove MGT,[4] and to a growing body of research on estimating the prevalence of MGT on Wikipedia (Brooks et al., 2024; Huang et al., 2025b).

Prior work on benchmarking MGT detectors (e.g., Guo et al., 2023; Li et al., 2023; Wang et al., 2023, 2024a) has included the Wikipedia domain but typically fails to reflect the complexities of editor-driven MGT instances on the platform. Existing experimental setups generally assume that MGT on Wikipedia results from (*i*) open-ended, topic-to-text generation and (*ii*) simplistic prompting techniques. These setups usually rely on a single prompt to generate an entire article, which diverges significantly from real-world Wikipedia editing practices that are task-specific and incremental. In fact, prompting an LLM to verbatim *"Write a Wikipedia article about [...],"* as done in earlier work, is explicitly discouraged by the community.[5]

These limitations in existing setups may obscure the actual performance of state-of-the-art (SOTA) detectors when applied to real-world Wikipedia contexts. Figure 2 shows that the textual characteristics of task-specific MGT—unlike open-ended, topic-to-text MGT—more closely resemble their human-written text (HWT) references. Detectors trained and evaluated on generic generation tasks may learn high-level textual patterns that are less transferable to task-specific MGT instances. Consequently, detectors may not generalise well to detecting diverse, task-specific MGT on Wikipedia, leaving an unknown number of instances with potentially harmful characteristics—such as hallucination or bias—largely undetected. To address this issue, we advocate for evaluating detectors on data that reflect practical use cases of editors integrating LLMs into their editorial workflows. This is essential for understanding the capacity of automatic detection methods to safeguard Wikipedia's knowledge integrity and to assist editors in identifying and removing low-quality MGT.

To this end, we build an MGT detection benchmark for *task-specific editing* scenarios on Wikipedia. To create our benchmark, we construct and release two new Wikipedia text corpora covering three languages with varying resource availability, enabling conclusions beyond the predominantly studied English Wikipedia. We then propose three editing tasks—*Paragraph Writing*, *Summarisation*, and *Text Style Transfer*—grounded in practical use cases identified by Ford et al. (2023), who analysed Wikipedia editors' perceived opportunities for LLM-assisted editing. For each task, we test various prompting techniques, generate MGT using diverse LLMs, and benchmark SOTA detectors across languages, generators, and tasks (see Figure 1). We hope that our multipurpose datasets will benefit the broader Wikipedia and AI communities in areas such as multilingual bias detection and single-document summarisation. We further aim to offer insights into the feasibility and reliability of automated detection methods for identifying MGT on Wikipedia.

Our contributions are as follows:

- We build two datasets for our benchmark covering English, Portuguese, and Vietnamese: **WikiPS**, a large-scale collection of high-quality (*i*) lead–infobox–body triplets and (*ii*) paragraphs; and **mWNC**, an extension of the WNC (Pryzant et al., 2020) to Portuguese and Vietnamese, and one of the first to include paragraph-level pairs for English.
- **W**ikipedia **E**diting **T**asks **B**enchmark, a comprehensive benchmark of 101,940 *task-specific* human-written and machine-generated Wikipedia texts, comprising three languages with varying levels of resource availability, four generators from two model families, and eight SOTA detectors from three detection families. We release all data and code on GitHub and plan to extend the benchmark with additional tasks, languages, and generators.
- We benchmark SOTA detectors on our data and find that detectors across all families struggle across tasks. While training-based detectors consistently outperform zero-shot meth-

[3]https://en.wikipedia.org/wiki/Wikipedia:Core_content_policies

[4]https://en.wikipedia.org/wiki/Wikipedia:WikiProject_AI_Cleanup

[5]https://en.wikipedia.org/wiki/Wikipedia:Large_language_models

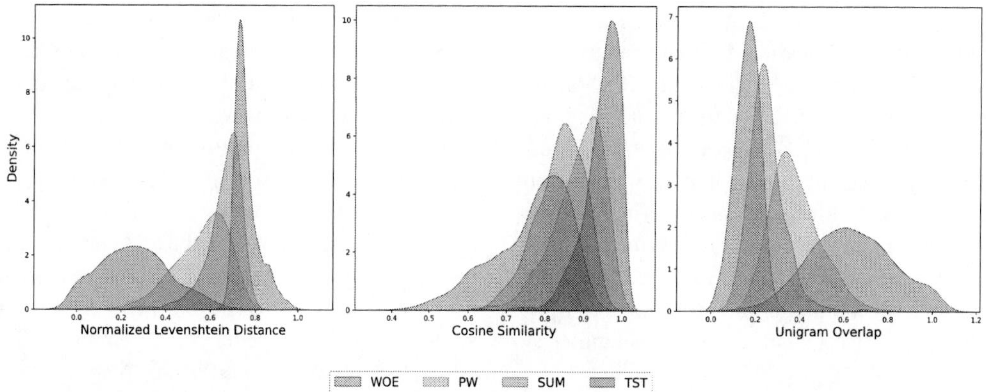

Figure 2: Comparison of MGT and HWT (N=600) for English Wikipedia Open-Ended Generation (WOE) vs. our Wikipedia editing tasks: Paragraph Writing (PW), Summarisation (SUM), and Text Style Transfer (TST). Task-specific MGT consistently demonstrates closer proximity to human writing across all dimensions.

ods, we observe substantial performance variation across languages, generators, and tasks.

2 Related Work

Wikipedia Editing Tasks We concentrate on three common editing tasks with varying degrees of LLM involvement: Paragraph Writing, Summarisation, and Text Style Transfer.

Paragraph Writing Generating new, encyclopaedic content—such as full paragraphs—is central to expanding knowledge on Wikipedia. This includes writing paragraphs from scratch, expanding article stubs, or rewriting existing content. With nearly half of all Wikipedia articles classified as stubs, researchers have extensively studied Wikipedia content generation.[6] The scope of generated content varies from paragraph-level (e.g., Liu et al., 2018; Balepur et al., 2023; Qian et al., 2023) to full-article generation (e.g., Sauper and Barzilay, 2009; Banerjee and Mitra, 2015; Fan and Gardent, 2022; Shao et al., 2024; Zhang et al., 2025). The methods employed range from early template-based approaches (Sauper and Barzilay, 2009) to more recent work using retrieval-augmented generation (RAG) with pre-trained language models (PLMs) (Fan and Gardent, 2022) or LLMs (Shao et al., 2024; Zhang et al., 2025).

Summarisation According to Wikipedia's Manual of Style,[7] each article should begin with a lead section that serves as an introduction by summarising its most important points. The literature treats lead section generation either as a multi-document (e.g., Liu et al., 2018; Ghalandari et al., 2020; Hayashi et al., 2021) or single-document (e.g., Casola et al., 2021; Gao et al., 2021; Perez-Beltrachini and Lapata, 2022; Sakota et al., 2023) summarisation problem. A model's objective is typically abstractive summarisation, that is, generating a lead section from scratch based on the article body.

Text Style Transfer Maintaining a Neutral Point of View[8] (NPOV) is a core Wikipedia policy, which states that all content must be written from a perspective that is fair, proportionate, and, as far as possible, free from editorial bias. Pryzant et al. (2020) introduce the Wikipedia Neutrality Corpus (WNC), a large-scale parallel corpus of biased and neutralised sentence pairs retrieved from NPOV-related revisions. They further introduce the task of *neutralisation*, a text style transfer task that aims to reduce subjectivity in a sentence while preserving its meaning. Recent work has used the WNC to improve data quality (Zhong et al., 2021), test generalisation to other domains (Salas-Jimenez et al., 2024), or examine the ability of LLMs to detect and neutralise bias (Ashkinaze et al., 2024).

MGT Detection Benchmarks There has been extensive work on benchmarking SOTA MGT detectors across diverse domains, languages, and generators. TuringBench (Uchendu et al., 2021) is one of the first benchmarks to study the Turing test and authorship attribution, using multiple generators in the news domain. MULTITuDE (Macko

[6]https://en.wikipedia.org/wiki/Wikipedia:Stub

[7]https://en.wikipedia.org/wiki/Wikipedia:Manual_of_Style

[8]https://en.wikipedia.org/wiki/Wikipedia:Neutral_point_of_view

et al., 2023) expands MGT data for languages other than English, testing detectors in multilingual settings. MAGE (Li et al., 2023) covers multiple domains, generators, and detectors, benchmarked across eight increasingly challenging detection scenarios. M4 (Wang et al., 2023) comprehensively includes various generators, languages, and domains, while M4GT (Wang et al., 2024b) expands on M4 by incorporating additional languages and introducing human-machine mixed detection. A recent line of work focuses on evading detectors through adversarial attacks (e.g., He et al., 2024; Wu et al., 2024; Zheng et al., 2025).

Most prior work has treated MGT generation primarily (*i*) as an open-ended text task, (*ii*) left different prompting techniques unexplored, and (*iii*) produced full articles with a single prompt. CUDRT (Tao et al., 2024) is a notable exception addressing (*i*) by introducing a bilingual, multi-domain benchmark that covers five types of LLM operations. However, it does not consider Wikipedia, lacks analysis of how different prompting techniques affect these operations, and is limited to only three detectors.

3 Dataset Construction

We construct two corpora for three languages with varying resource levels: English (high), Portuguese (medium), and Vietnamese (low). **WikiPS** includes paragraphs and lead–content pairs. **mWNC** is a multilingual version of the WNC (Pryzant et al., 2020). Appendix A provides detailed descriptions of the dataset construction, and Appendix Table 6 presents dataset statistics.

3.1 WikiPS

We construct **Wiki**pedia **P**aragraphs and **S**ummarisation, a large-scale collection of Wikipedia paragraphs and lead–content pairs. To ensure that our data is not contaminated by MGT, we use the latest versions of all mainspace articles prior to the release of ChatGPT on 30 November 2022. For each language, we randomly retrieve 100,000 non-stub articles from the MediaWiki Action API,[9] apply extensive filtering and cleaning of the HTML, and parse the lead section, infobox, paragraphs, and references. This forms our article-level base sample, from which we construct the paragraph and summarisation subsets, respectively.

[9] https://www.mediawiki.org/wiki/API:Main_page

Paragraphs For each language, we consider all paragraphs from 20,000 articles in our base sample. To ensure paragraph quality, we retain only those that contain at least three sentences and 20 characters, include at least one reference, and have word counts within two standard deviations of the respective sample mean. We also add diverse metadata, such as the paragraph's location on the page, to enable filtering for specific types of paragraphs.

Summarisation We retrieve lead–infobox–body triplets from all articles in each language, as information in the lead section is often sourced from the infobox (Gao et al., 2021). If an infobox is not available, we still extract the article, leaving the infobox field empty. We then merge the infobox (if present) and article body with minimal formatting into lead–content pairs. For English and Portuguese, we exclude pairs in which the lead/content is shorter than 10/100 characters, respectively, or longer than two standard deviations above the sample mean. For Vietnamese, we adjust the upper context limit to a minimum of 2,900 words due to its considerably longer articles. Appendix Table 7 compares our dataset to commonly used summarisation datasets.

3.2 mWNC

multilingual **WNC** extends the original WNC (Pryzant et al., 2020), which consists of English biased–neutralised sentence pairs, by adding pairs for Portuguese and Vietnamese, as well as paragraph-level pairs for English. We primarily follow the methodology of Pryzant et al. (2020), including crawling NPOV-related revisions, aligning pre- and post-neutralisation sentences, and applying rule-based filtering to improve precision. However, we modify their procedure by relaxing certain constraints to increase the number of instances for the Vietnamese Wikipedia, where the number of NPOV-related revisions is comparatively low. Furthermore, we are among the first to collect biased–neutralised paragraph-level pairs. We identify biased–neutralised paragraph pairs if three or more adjacent sentences each contain at least one NPOV-related edit. Due to the considerably smaller number of NPOV-related revisions in the other languages, we were only able to produce paragraph-level data for English.

4 Editing Tasks Design

We define three editing tasks with varying degrees of LLM intervention: *Paragraph Writing*, *Summarisation*, and *Text Style Transfer*. These tasks are empirically motivated by Ford et al. (2023), who found that Wikipedia editors see potential in LLMs for *generating article drafts or stubs*, *summarising content*, and *improving language*. We implement Paragraph Writing and Summarisation using the WikiPS corpus, and Text Style Transfer using the mWNC.

For each task and language, we evaluate three prompting strategies on a length-stratified 10% sample of the target data using GPT-4o mini,[10] and select the best-performing prompt to generate MGT for our benchmark. Appendix B provides implementation details and prompt templates.

4.1 Paragraph Writing

We define *Paragraph Writing* as the task of writing the opening paragraph of a new section, resembling a scenario in which an editor aims to add new content to an article. In contrast to prior work on open-ended generation (e.g., Guo et al., 2023; Li et al., 2023; Wang et al., 2023, 2024a), we frame this as a *content-conditioned* generation task, where the model receives additional information about the content and style of the output. This *content creation* task involves the highest degree of LLM contribution, as the model generates the paragraph from scratch.

We devise three prompts with increasing levels of content conditioning. **Minimal** simply instructs the model to write a paragraph given article and section titles. We include this prompt as it reflects generation settings in prior work and thus serves as a comparative baseline. **Content Prompts** expand Minimal by incorporating up to ten content prompts about the target HWT paragraph (e.g., "What is London's population?"), obtained from GPT-4o,[11] to steer the model towards factual alignment with the HWT reference. Lastly, to enhance the factual accuracy of the generated text, we implement a web-based search **Naive RAG** (Gao et al., 2024), which adds relevant context to the Content Prompts. Appendix B.1.3 provides implementation details of Naive RAG.

We evaluate these prompts using standard automatic metrics: BLEU (Papineni et al., 2002) and ROUGE (Lin, 2004) for n-gram overlap, BERTScore (Zhang et al., 2019) for semantic similarity, and QAFactEval (Fabbri et al., 2022) (F1-score) as a QA-based metric for factual consistency between HWT and MGT.[12]

Language	Technique	BLEU	ROUGE-1	ROUGE-2	ROUGE-L	BERTScore	QAFactEval
English	Minimal	0.02	0.29	0.06	0.17	0.76	0.06
	Content Prompts	0.22	0.57	0.31	0.44	**0.88**	0.25
	RAG	**0.25**	**0.61**	**0.35**	**0.47**	**0.88**	**0.38**
Portuguese	Minimal	0.02	0.31	0.06	0.17	0.86	0.06
	Content Prompts	0.20	0.56	0.30	0.41	0.91	0.25
	RAG	**0.25**	**0.61**	**0.37**	**0.47**	**0.92**	**0.42**
Vietnamese	Minimal	0.04	0.67	0.26	0.32	0.85	0.06
	Content Prompts	0.28	0.78	0.52	0.54	0.91	0.27
	RAG	**0.30**	**0.79**	**0.54**	**0.55**	**0.92**	**0.36**

Table 1: Paragraph Writing prompts evaluation results.

Table 1 presents our prompting evaluation results. We find that our Naive RAG approach consistently outperforms both Minimal and Content Prompts across subtasks and languages. The low evaluation scores for Minimal prompts highlight that MGT produced in prior work is often synthetically divergent from its human-written references. While Content Prompts substantially improve performance, Naive RAG further enhances generation quality, particularly in terms of factual consistency, which is critical for encyclopaedic content.[13] Based on these findings, we adopt Naive RAG as the prompting strategy for the Paragraph Writing task in our MGT detection experiments.

4.2 Summarisation

Summarisation tasks the model with generating a lead section of comparable length to the human-written reference, based on the article's body and infobox, both of which are the main sources for lead section information (Gao et al., 2021). We frame this as a single-document, abstractive summarisation task, following Wikipedia's Manual of Style[14] and prior work on Wikipedia summarisation (Casola et al., 2021; Gao et al., 2021; Perez-Beltrachini and Lapata, 2022). Compared to *Paragraph Writing*, this *content condensation* task involves slightly less LLM contribution due to its stronger grounding in existing article content.

We use three prompting techniques from the literature on LLM-generated summaries (Goyal et al., 2022; Pu et al., 2023; Zhang et al., 2023) that align

[10] https://platform.openai.com/docs/models/gpt-4o-mini

[11] https://openai.com/index/gpt-4o-system-card/

[12] For Portuguese and Vietnamese texts, QAFactEval evaluations were performed using GPT-4 translations.

[13] https://en.wikipedia.org/wiki/Wikipedia:Verifiability

[14] https://en.wikipedia.org/wiki/Wikipedia:Manual_of_Style/Lead_section

with this editing scenario. Each prompt contains the article content as input and conditions the output length on the target lead length. **Minimal** is a simple zero-shot baseline prompt that instructs the model to summarise the article content. **Instruction** adds a concise definition of, and instructions for compiling, a lead section to guide the model more explicitly. **Few-shot** further includes 1–3 high-quality lead–content examples, retrieved from the respective Wikipedia Featured Articles page, in addition to the Instruction prompt to enable in-context learning (Brown et al., 2020).[15] We evaluate these prompts using traditional automatic metrics for summarisation evaluation (see Section 4.1).

Language	Technique	BLEU	ROUGE-1	ROUGE-2	ROUGE-L	BERTScore	QAFactEval
English	Minimal	0.06	0.37	0.13	0.26	0.79	0.45
	Instruction	0.13	0.44	0.21	0.33	0.82	**0.46**
	One-shot	**0.18**	**0.47**	**0.24**	**0.36**	**0.83**	**0.46**
	Two-shot	**0.18**	**0.47**	**0.24**	**0.36**	**0.83**	**0.46**
	Three-shot	0.16	0.46	0.23	0.35	**0.83**	**0.46**
Portuguese	Minimal	0.06	0.35	0.13	0.23	0.87	**0.48**
	Instruction	**0.11**	0.42	0.19	0.30	**0.88**	**0.48**
	One-shot	**0.11**	0.42	0.19	0.29	**0.88**	**0.48**
	Two-shot	**0.11**	**0.43**	0.19	**0.30**	**0.88**	0.47
	Three-shot	0.12	**0.43**	**0.20**	**0.30**	**0.88**	0.47
Vietnamese	Minimal	0.07	0.63	0.28	0.35	0.86	**0.45**
	Instruction	0.11	0.64	0.31	**0.38**	**0.87**	0.43
	One-shot	**0.12**	0.65	**0.32**	**0.38**	**0.87**	**0.45**
	Two-shot	**0.12**	**0.66**	**0.32**	**0.38**	**0.87**	0.44
	Three-shot	0.11	0.65	**0.32**	**0.38**	**0.87**	0.42

Table 2: Summarisation prompts evaluation results.

Table 2 presents the summarisation prompt evaluation results, showing that across languages, Instruction and Few-shot achieve higher overlap and semantic similarity scores, although Few-shot only marginally improves over Instruction. Factuality scores remain relatively stable across prompts, presumably because summarisation is a core task in aligning LLMs through reinforcement learning from human feedback (Ouyang et al., 2022). Given that increasing the number of shots does not yield further improvements, and considering the context window of smaller LLMs, we select one-shot prompting for our experiments.

4.3 Text Style Transfer

We adopt the TST task of *neutralising* revision-level NPOV violations, as introduced by Pryzant et al. (2020). In our setup, the model is instructed to revise a biased sentence or paragraph with minimal edits, aligning the output with Wikipedia's neutrality guidelines. While various TST tasks are possible on Wikipedia, focusing on NPOV violations ensures direct alignment with one of its core content policies.[16] This *content modification* task involves the least LLM contribution, as the model is conditioned to perform only minor revisions to existing text.

We test three prompting techniques for TST that are conceptually identical to those used in summarisation and align with recent work on LLM-based TST (Reif et al., 2021; Dwivedi-Yu et al., 2022; Ashkinaze et al., 2024). All prompts include the biased input text and constrain the output to be no longer than the target text. Compared to summarisation, **Minimal** instructs the model to neutralise the input; **Instruction** adds a concise definition of Wikipedia's NPOV policy; and **Few-shot** includes 1–5 randomly sampled biased–neutralised examples.

We evaluate these TST prompts along two dimensions: *semantic content preservation*, for which we report BLEU (Papineni et al., 2002), ROUGE (Lin, 2004), and BERTScore (Zhang et al., 2019); and *style transfer accuracy*, for which we fine-tune pre-trained language models for each language and report the accuracy of binary style classification. Fine-tuning details are provided in Appendix B.3.

Language	Technique	BLEU	ROUGE-1	ROUGE-2	ROUGE-L	BERTScore	ST
English	Minimal	0.35	0.68	0.52	0.66	0.92	0.90
	Instruction	0.36	0.68	0.52	0.66	0.92	**0.94**
	One-shot	0.52	0.78	0.65	0.76	**0.95**	0.91
	Two-shot	0.47	0.75	0.61	0.73	0.94	0.90
	Three-shot	0.54	0.79	0.67	0.78	**0.95**	0.89
	Four-shot	**0.56**	**0.80**	**0.69**	**0.79**	**0.95**	0.89
	Five-shot	**0.55**	**0.80**	0.68	0.78	**0.95**	0.91
Portuguese	Minimal	0.41	0.71	0.58	0.69	0.94	0.86
	Instruction	0.40	0.70	0.57	0.67	0.94	0.88
	One-shot	0.50	0.75	0.64	0.74	**0.96**	0.90
	Two-shot	0.51	0.77	0.65	0.75	**0.96**	0.89
	Three-shot	0.53	0.78	0.66	0.76	**0.96**	0.91
	Four-shot	**0.58**	**0.81**	**0.70**	**0.79**	**0.96**	**0.92**
	Five-shot	0.55	0.79	0.68	0.77	**0.96**	0.91
Vietnamese	Minimal	0.43	0.78	0.65	0.73	0.95	0.84
	Instruction	0.45	0.80	0.67	0.73	0.94	0.79
	One-shot	0.44	0.78	0.66	0.71	0.95	**0.88**
	Two-shot	0.51	0.82	0.70	0.76	0.95	0.87
	Three-shot	0.50	0.81	0.70	0.75	0.95	0.85
	Four-shot	0.51	0.82	0.70	0.76	0.95	0.85
	Five-shot	**0.55**	**0.83**	**0.73**	**0.78**	**0.96**	0.84
English Para.	Minimal	0.35	0.68	0.52	0.66	0.92	0.97
	Instruction	0.36	0.68	0.52	0.66	0.92	**0.99**
	One-shot	0.52	0.78	0.65	0.76	**0.95**	0.95
	Two-shot	0.47	0.75	0.61	0.73	0.94	0.98
	Three-shot	0.54	0.79	0.67	0.78	**0.95**	0.96
	Four-shot	**0.56**	**0.80**	**0.69**	**0.79**	**0.95**	0.95
	Five-shot	0.55	**0.80**	0.68	0.78	**0.95**	0.96

Table 3: TST prompts evaluation results.

Table 3 presents the prompt evaluation metrics for the TST task, evaluated at the sentence level for all languages, and additionally at the paragraph level for English. Across languages and levels, we find that four- and five-shot prompting consistently outperforms Minimal and Instruction

[15] https://en.wikipedia.org/wiki/Wikipedia:Featured_articles

[16] https://en.wikipedia.org/wiki/Wikipedia:Neutral_point_of_view

prompts. While differences in semantic similarity and style transfer are marginal across prompts, we observe substantial improvements in overlap-based metrics as the number of few-shot examples increases. These improvements can be attributed to the fact that neutralisation edits in mWNC tend to be relatively minimal. For instance, in the English sentence subset, on average only 14% of words are deleted and 7% added—similar trends hold for the other subsets. As a result, the model appears to learn from the examples to apply similarly sparse edits, thereby producing outputs that match the reference text more closely in terms of n-gram overlap. Based on these findings, we adopt five-shot prompting to generate MGT in our subsequent experiments.

5 Experimental Setup

In this section, we introduce generators, detectors, benchmark construction, and evaluation metrics.

Generators We generate MGT using four multilingual models from two families: proprietary and open-weight. We select models based on their ranking at the time of writing on LM Arena,[17] an open-source platform for crowdsourced AI benchmarking. For proprietary models, we use **GPT-4o mini**[18] and **Gemini 2.0 Flash**.[19] For open-weight models, we select **Qwen2.5-7B-Instruct**[20] and **Mistral-7B-Instruct**.[21] We opt for smaller models in this category to better align with our editor-driven writing task scenarios.

Detectors We evaluate six detectors from three different families: training-based, zero-shot white-box, and zero-shot black-box methods. We consider only multilingual LLMs for all families. Specifically, we use **XLM-RoBERTa** (Conneau et al., 2020) and **mDeBERTa** (He et al., 2023) as training-based detectors, which we fine-tune with hyperparameter search; **Binoculars** (Hans et al., 2024), **LLR** (Su et al., 2023), and **FastDetect-GPT (White-Box)** (Hans et al., 2024) as zero-shot white-box detectors; and **Revise-Detect** (Zhu et al., 2023a), **GECScore** (Wu et al., 2025), and **Fast-DetectGPT (Black-Box)** (Hans et al., 2024) as zero-shot black-box detectors. Appendix C provides an overview and implementation details of each detector.

WETBench We construct our benchmarking data by randomly sampling 2,700 HWT per task from the corresponding subsets of WikiPS and mWNC. For Paragraph Writing and Summarisation, we balance each subset by length tertiles; for TST, we evaluate at the sentence level for all languages and at the paragraph level for English only. For each task–language subset, we generate MGT using the four generators introduced above, applying the best-performing prompts from our prompt evaluation in Section 4: Naive RAG for Paragraph Writing, one-shot prompting for Summarisation, and five-shot prompting for TST. Our benchmark corpus comprises 101,940 human- and machine-written texts across tasks, languages, and generators. Appendix Table 6 presents benchmark statistics.

Evaluation Metrics Given the parallel nature of our benchmark data, our main evaluation metric is accuracy. We additionally report F1-scores, which represent the weighted harmonic mean of precision and recall.

6 Results

Table 4 presents our benchmarking results. Our main results are: (*i*) our benchmark challenges detectors, which achieve considerably lower scores than in prior work (e.g., Macko et al., 2023; Guo et al., 2023; Li et al., 2023; Wang et al., 2023, 2024a), (*ii*) supervised detectors significantly outperform zero-shot methods across all tasks and languages, and (*iii*) detection accuracy is highest for summarisation, followed by slightly lower accuracy for paragraph writing, and lowest for TST. The following presents the most relevant trends by task.

Paragraph Writing Across languages and models, training-based detectors outperform zero-shot methods by 19–30% accuracy on average. Black-box detectors are 3–6% more accurate than white-box detectors in English and Portuguese but perform slightly worse in Vietnamese. Only white-box detectors show a slight increase in accuracy when moving from high- to low-resource languages.

[17] https://blog.lmarena.ai/
[18] https://openai.com/index/gpt-4o-mini-advancing-cost-efficient-intelligence/
[19] https://deepmind.google/technologies/gemini/flash/
[20] https://huggingface.co/Qwen/Qwen2.5-7B-Instruct
[21] https://huggingface.co/mistralai/Mistral-7B-Instruct-v0.3

English

Task	Detector	GPT-4o mini		Gemini 2.0		Qwen 2.5		Mistral		Avg	
		ACC	F1	ACC	F1	ACC	F1	ACC	F1	ACC	F1
Introductory Paragraph	Binoculars	0.61	0.60	0.58	0.61	0.60	0.58	0.55	0.63	0.59	0.60
	LLR	0.52	0.51	0.50	0.67	0.50	0.67	0.53	0.62	0.51	0.62
	FDGPT (WB)	0.59	0.60	0.54	0.52	0.52	0.43	0.52	0.52	0.54	0.51
	Avg. White-box	0.57	0.57	0.54	0.60	0.54	0.56	0.54	0.59	0.55	0.58
	Revise	0.53	0.41	0.53	0.50	0.52	0.55	0.52	0.62	0.52	0.52
	GECScore	0.82	0.82	0.77	0.75	0.77	0.75	0.72	0.73	0.77	0.76
	FDGPT (BB)	0.58	0.61	0.53	0.49	0.52	0.45	0.54	0.50	0.55	0.51
	Avg. Black-box	0.64	0.61	0.61	0.58	0.60	0.58	0.59	0.62	0.61	0.60
	xlm-RoBERTa	0.81	0.81	0.84	0.84	0.85	0.85	0.83	0.83	0.83	0.83
	mDeBERTa	0.86	0.86	0.84	0.83	0.89	0.88	0.90	0.89	0.87	0.87
	Avg. Supervised	0.84	0.83	0.84	0.84	0.87	0.87	0.86	0.86	0.85	0.85
Summarisation	Binoculars	0.60	0.60	0.62	0.58	0.62	0.62	0.62	0.69	0.61	0.62
	LLR	0.52	0.65	0.52	0.64	0.54	0.66	0.61	0.68	0.55	0.66
	FDGPT (WB)	0.60	0.59	0.60	0.59	0.55	0.51	0.61	0.60	0.59	0.57
	Avg. White-box	0.57	0.61	0.58	0.61	0.57	0.60	0.61	0.66	0.58	0.62
	Revise	0.53	0.61	0.53	0.58	0.53	0.62	0.53	0.61	0.53	0.60
	GECScore	0.80	0.81	0.71	0.70	0.75	0.75	0.74	0.76	0.75	0.75
	FDGPT (BB)	0.59	0.58	0.59	0.63	0.56	0.60	0.63	0.62	0.59	0.61
	Avg. Black-box	0.64	0.66	0.61	0.63	0.61	0.66	0.63	0.66	0.62	0.65
	xlm-RoBERTa	0.92	0.92	0.86	0.85	0.95	0.95	0.90	0.90	0.91	0.90
	mDeBERTa	0.91	0.91	0.83	0.83	0.93	0.93	0.91	0.90	0.89	0.89
	Avg. Supervised	0.91	0.91	0.84	0.84	0.94	0.94	0.90	0.90	0.90	0.90
Text Style Transfer	Binoculars	0.53	0.46	0.52	0.33	0.50	0.05	0.53	0.54	0.52	0.34
	LLR	0.50	0.02	0.50	0.05	0.50	0.02	0.50	0.04	0.50	0.03
	FDGPT (WB)	0.54	0.55	0.53	0.54	0.50	0.67	0.53	0.54	0.52	0.57
	Avg. White-box	0.52	0.34	0.52	0.31	0.50	0.24	0.52	0.37	0.51	0.32
	Revise	0.53	0.63	0.52	0.60	0.52	0.65	0.52	0.62	0.52	0.62
	GECScore	0.65	0.64	0.62	0.59	0.64	0.62	0.62	0.60	0.63	0.61
	FDGPT (BB)	0.53	0.55	0.51	0.49	0.50	0.01	0.53	0.52	0.52	0.39
	Avg. Black-box	0.57	0.61	0.55	0.56	0.55	0.42	0.56	0.58	0.56	0.54
	xlm-RoBERTa	0.64	0.59	0.59	0.57	0.59	0.58	0.64	0.61	0.61	0.59
	mDeBERTa	0.62	0.58	0.60	0.60	0.58	0.58	0.62	0.62	0.61	0.59
	Avg. Supervised	0.63	0.59	0.60	0.59	0.59	0.58	0.63	0.62	0.61	0.59

Portuguese

Task	Detector	GPT-4o mini		Gemini 2.0		Qwen 2.5		Mistral		Avg	
		ACC	F1	ACC	F1	ACC	F1	ACC	F1	ACC	F1
Introductory Paragraph	Binoculars	0.68	0.66	0.64	0.64	0.64	0.60	0.54	0.61	0.62	0.63
	LLR	0.57	0.51	0.54	0.51	0.50	0.67	0.53	0.51	0.53	0.55
	FDGPT (WB)	0.68	0.66	0.63	0.63	0.56	0.53	0.52	0.57	0.60	0.60
	Avg. White-box	0.64	0.61	0.60	0.59	0.56	0.60	0.53	0.56	0.58	0.59
	Revise	0.55	0.58	0.56	0.50	0.54	0.53	0.52	0.59	0.54	0.55
	GECScore	0.79	0.79	0.80	0.80	0.65	0.66	0.54	0.66	0.69	0.73
	FDGPT (BB)	0.69	0.66	0.62	0.60	0.56	0.44	0.54	0.42	0.60	0.53
	Avg. Black-box	0.68	0.68	0.66	0.63	0.58	0.54	0.53	0.56	0.61	0.60
	xlm-RoBERTa	0.76	0.75	0.80	0.79	0.83	0.82	0.76	0.74	0.79	0.78
	mDeBERTa	0.76	0.74	0.80	0.79	0.84	0.83	0.85	0.85	0.81	0.80
	Avg. Supervised	0.76	0.75	0.80	0.79	0.83	0.83	0.80	0.79	0.80	0.79
Summarisation	Binoculars	0.72	0.73	0.70	0.72	0.71	0.72	0.62	0.66	0.69	0.71
	LLR	0.58	0.57	0.56	0.54	0.54	0.65	0.55	0.67	0.56	0.61
	FDGPT (WB)	0.72	0.70	0.69	0.69	0.65	0.63	0.56	0.58	0.65	0.65
	Avg. White-box	0.67	0.67	0.65	0.65	0.63	0.67	0.58	0.64	0.63	0.66
	Revise	0.54	0.51	0.53	0.57	0.53	0.55	0.51	0.63	0.53	0.56
	GECScore	0.78	0.79	0.73	0.72	0.68	0.70	0.52	0.64	0.68	0.71
	FDGPT (BB)	0.71	0.69	0.67	0.70	0.65	0.66	0.57	0.57	0.65	0.65
	Avg. Black-box	0.67	0.66	0.64	0.66	0.62	0.63	0.53	0.61	0.62	0.64
	xlm-RoBERTa	0.91	0.91	0.84	0.84	0.91	0.91	0.94	0.94	0.90	0.90
	mDeBERTa	0.89	0.89	0.86	0.85	0.94	0.93	0.94	0.94	0.91	0.90
	Avg. Supervised	0.90	0.90	0.85	0.85	0.92	0.92	0.94	0.94	0.90	0.90
Text Style Transfer	Binoculars	0.56	0.54	0.55	0.51	0.53	0.49	0.52	0.48	0.54	0.51
	LLR	0.51	0.25	0.50	0.03	0.50	0.02	0.50	0.32	0.50	0.15
	FDGPT (WB)	0.56	0.53	0.54	0.51	0.51	0.44	0.51	0.49	0.53	0.49
	Avg. White-box	0.54	0.44	0.53	0.35	0.51	0.32	0.51	0.43	0.52	0.38
	Revise	0.53	0.56	0.52	0.59	0.52	0.53	0.51	0.59	0.52	0.56
	GECScore	0.66	0.63	0.62	0.59	0.61	0.60	0.55	0.54	0.61	0.59
	FDGPT (BB)	0.55	0.57	0.53	0.52	0.51	0.22	0.52	0.32	0.53	0.41
	Avg. Black-box	0.58	0.59	0.56	0.57	0.55	0.45	0.52	0.48	0.55	0.52
	xlm-RoBERTa	0.63	0.60	0.66	0.65	0.58	0.58	0.68	0.67	0.64	0.63
	mDeBERTa	0.64	0.58	0.68	0.68	0.66	0.66	0.69	0.69	0.67	0.65
	Avg. Supervised	0.63	0.59	0.67	0.67	0.62	0.62	0.68	0.68	0.65	0.64

Vietnamese

Task	Detector	GPT-4o mini		Gemini 2.0		Qwen 2.5		Mistral		Avg	
		ACC	F1	ACC	F1	ACC	F1	ACC	F1	ACC	F1
Introductory Paragraph	Binoculars	0.77	0.77	0.72	0.72	0.70	0.66	0.50	0.67	0.67	0.70
	LLR	0.63	0.60	0.58	0.54	0.51	0.19	0.50	0.00	0.56	0.33
	FDGPT (WB)	0.76	0.77	0.70	0.69	0.59	0.53	0.50	0.00	0.64	0.50
	Avg. White-box	0.72	0.71	0.67	0.65	0.60	0.46	0.50	0.22	0.62	0.51
	Revise	0.53	0.50	0.54	0.56	0.54	0.59	0.50	0.00	0.53	0.41
	GECScore	0.72	0.70	0.70	0.70	0.58	0.47	0.50	0.67	0.62	0.63
	FDGPT (BB)	0.74	0.74	0.68	0.70	0.59	0.59	0.50	0.00	0.63	0.51
	Avg. Black-box	0.66	0.65	0.64	0.65	0.57	0.55	0.50	0.22	0.59	0.52
	xlm-RoBERTa	0.75	0.72	0.82	0.81	0.89	0.89	0.98	0.98	0.86	0.85
	mDeBERTa	0.77	0.76	0.82	0.81	0.87	0.87	0.98	0.98	0.86	0.86
	Avg. Supervised	0.76	0.74	0.82	0.81	0.88	0.88	0.98	0.98	0.86	0.85
Summarisation	Binoculars	0.72	0.72	0.70	0.71	0.72	0.73	0.50	0.67	0.66	0.71
	LLR	0.58	0.47	0.55	0.47	0.54	0.65	0.51	0.67	0.55	0.56
	FDGPT (WB)	0.73	0.72	0.71	0.71	0.64	0.62	0.50	0.00	0.64	0.51
	Avg. White-box	0.68	0.64	0.66	0.63	0.64	0.67	0.50	0.45	0.62	0.59
	Revise	0.53	0.57	0.54	0.56	0.54	0.56	0.50	0.66	0.53	0.59
	GECScore	0.71	0.70	0.67	0.66	0.63	0.64	0.50	0.67	0.63	0.67
	FDGPT (BB)	0.70	0.68	0.68	0.66	0.64	0.61	0.50	0.01	0.63	0.49
	Avg. Black-box	0.65	0.65	0.63	0.63	0.60	0.60	0.50	0.45	0.60	0.58
	xlm-RoBERTa	0.86	0.86	0.78	0.77	0.94	0.93	0.94	0.94	0.88	0.87
	mDeBERTa	0.84	0.84	0.77	0.76	0.90	0.90	0.96	0.96	0.87	0.87
	Avg. Supervised	0.85	0.85	0.78	0.76	0.92	0.91	0.95	0.95	0.87	0.87
Text Style Transfer	Binoculars	0.59	0.55	0.57	0.52	0.53	0.47	0.50	0.00	0.55	0.39
	LLR	0.52	0.29	0.51	0.16	0.51	0.26	0.50	0.67	0.51	0.34
	FDGPT (WB)	0.58	0.57	0.55	0.55	0.53	0.52	0.50	0.00	0.54	0.41
	Avg. White-box	0.56	0.47	0.54	0.41	0.52	0.42	0.50	0.22	0.53	0.38
	Revise	0.53	0.59	0.54	0.49	0.51	0.66	0.51	0.66	0.52	0.60
	GECScore	0.63	0.57	0.57	0.47	0.56	0.48	0.50	0.00	0.57	0.38
	FDGPT (BB)	0.57	0.53	0.53	0.46	0.52	0.51	0.50	0.00	0.53	0.37
	Avg. Black-box	0.58	0.56	0.55	0.47	0.53	0.55	0.50	0.22	0.54	0.45
	xlm-RoBERTa	0.63	0.62	0.68	0.68	0.54	0.52	0.52	0.45	0.59	0.57
	mDeBERTa	0.62	0.58	0.69	0.69	0.61	0.60	0.64	0.64	0.64	0.63
	Avg. Supervised	0.63	0.60	0.69	0.68	0.57	0.56	0.58	0.54	0.62	0.60

Table 4: Detection accuracy (ACC) and F1-scores (F1) across tasks, languages, and models. Gray highlights average performances across detector families by generator (rows) and across generators by detector (bold columns).

Within detector families, we do not find any substantial differences between the two training-based models. Among white-box detectors, Binoculars achieves up to 11% higher accuracy, with performance on low-resource languages approaching that of training-based methods. For black-box detectors, GECScore exhibits up to 25% higher accuracy compared to other models in its category.

Considering generators, training-based detectors achieve on average 2–7% higher accuracy on smaller-sized generators. This pattern is reversed for zero-shot detectors, where accuracy is higher for larger models, with the gap widening in lower-resource languages. These results suggest that when generating paragraphs from scratch, smaller models leave more detectable semantic and syntactic traces for training-based detectors. In contrast, the internals and token-level patterns of larger models seem to exhibit stronger signals than those of smaller models for zero-shot methods.

We observe substantial anomalies in Mistral's output for Vietnamese. The model often fails to follow prompts, producing unclear outputs that provide simple cues for training-based detectors but appear to confuse zero-shot methods. We provide an analysis of Mistral's generation issues in Appendix D.1.

Summarisation Among all tasks, supervised detectors perform best on summarisation, achieving an average accuracy of 89% across languages and generators. An exception is Gemini 2.0, for which detection accuracies are on average 6–17% lower, suggesting that its summaries may more closely resemble human-written references. While most LLMs are trained on summarisation tasks, enabling strong zero-shot performance (Ouyang et al., 2022), Wikipedia lead sections follow a distinctive style and formatting that seem to provide strong cues for training-based detectors.

Compared to Paragraph Writing, average detection accuracies for zero-shot models are slightly higher. White-box detectors achieve 4% higher accuracy on English summaries compared to black-box models, while performance is similar for Portuguese and Vietnamese. As in Paragraph Writing, Binoculars achieves the highest average accuracy (65%) among black-box detectors across languages and models, while GECScore performs best among white-box methods (68%).

In contrast to Paragraph Writing, zero-shot metrics show little variation across generators for English. However, for Portuguese and Vietnamese, a similar pattern emerges: summaries generated by larger models are slightly easier to detect. This effect is less pronounced than in Paragraph Writing, with an average accuracy difference of around 6%.

We attribute the similar trends between Paragraph Writing and Summarisation to the nature of both tasks: each involves generating text from scratch, conditioned either on retrieved context or article content. We observe the same issues as before for Mistral's Vietnamese summaries.

TST For sentence-level TST, we observe the lowest accuracy scores across all tasks and detector

Detector	TST English Paragraphs									
	GPT-4o mini		Gemini 2.0		Qwen 2.5		Mistral		Avg	
	ACC	F1	ACC	F1	ACC	F1	ACC	F1	ACC	F1
Binoculars	0.58	0.53	0.55	0.47	0.52	0.39	0.57	0.51	**0.56**	**0.48**
LLR	0.52	0.25	0.51	0.22	0.50	0.03	0.53	0.40	**0.51**	**0.22**
FDGPT (WB)	0.60	0.63	0.56	0.60	0.52	0.60	0.58	0.61	**0.56**	**0.61**
Avg (White-box)	0.57	0.47	0.54	0.43	0.52	0.34	0.56	0.51	**0.55**	**0.44**
Revise	0.53	0.62	0.52	0.56	0.53	0.42	0.52	0.55	**0.53**	**0.54**
GECScore	0.83	0.82	0.64	0.67	0.73	0.69	0.67	0.69	**0.72**	**0.72**
FDGPT (BB)	0.59	0.62	0.54	0.55	0.51	0.63	0.58	0.54	**0.56**	**0.59**
Avg (Black-box)	0.65	0.69	0.57	0.59	0.59	0.58	0.59	0.59	**0.60**	**0.61**
xlm-RoBERTa	0.78	0.77	0.78	0.77	0.78	0.77	0.71	0.71	**0.76**	**0.76**
mDeBERTa	0.83	0.83	0.77	0.76	0.81	0.81	0.67	0.64	**0.77**	**0.76**
Avg (Supervised)	0.81	0.80	0.78	0.77	0.80	0.79	0.69	0.67	**0.77**	**0.76**

Table 5: Detection accuracy (ACC) and F1-scores (F1) for TST English paragraphs. Gray highlights average performances across detector families by generator (rows) and across generators by detector (bold columns).

families. While zero-shot detectors average between 52–56% across languages and generators, training-based methods achieve only slightly higher scores, ranging from 61–65%. A notable exception is GECScore, which outperforms other zero-shot methods by up to 12%.

We attribute part of the reduced performance to the sentence-level setting. Comparing the English sentence-level results in Table 4 to the paragraph-level results in Table 5, we observe accuracy gains of up to 18%, depending on the model. However, these improvements mostly apply to white-box and training-based models.

Compared to Paragraph Writing and Summarisation, TST involves only minimal modifications to human-written text. While detection scores on English paragraphs are slightly lower than for full generation from scratch, they remain substantially higher than for sentence-level TST. This suggests that training-based detectors can identify similarly strong MGT signals in paragraph-level text, regardless of whether the content is generated from scratch or modified at the token level.

7 Conclusion

We present **WETBench**, a multilingual, multi-generator benchmark for detecting MGT in task-specific Wikipedia editing scenarios. We build the benchmark from two new large-scale, multilingual Wikipedia text corpora—**WikiPS** and **mWNC**—which support a range of tasks relevant to the Wikipedia and AI communities. Based on these data, we define three representative tasks, evaluate multiple prompting strategies, generate MGT from diverse LLMs using the best-performing prompts, and benchmark detectors.

Our benchmark reveals that detectors from diverse families underperform on our data, with substantial variation across languages, models, and tasks. Training-based detectors consistently outperform zero-shot methods but achieve only moderate detection accuracy. These results indicate that existing detectors struggle to generalise beyond generic setups, highlighting uncertainty around their reliability and effectiveness in real-world, editor-driven MGT scenarios on Wikipedia.

In future work, we plan to extend the benchmark with additional tasks, generators, and languages. We also aim to investigate the generalisability of our findings to open-ended generation tasks and other domains.

Limitations

Editing Task Selection We identify three common editing tasks, based on Ford et al. (2023), that vary in editing intensity. However, many other relevant editing tasks exist, reflecting different forms of content transformation. In particular, *text translation* is a critical use case across many language editions of Wikipedia, as it helps bridge content gaps. Given the increasing capabilities of LLMs in translation (Jiao et al., 2023; Zhu et al., 2023b; Yan et al., 2024), and the associated risks (see Section 1), detecting machine-generated translations is an important and underexplored task. Similarly, there are alternative approaches to TST, such as grammar and spelling correction, which are highly relevant, especially for non-native Wikipedia editors.

Real-World Relevance of Editing Tasks Our task selection is grounded in the study by Ford et al. (2023), which explores how Wikipedia editors perceive opportunities for AI-assisted writing. However, we acknowledge that our benchmark does not fully capture how MGT actually arises in real-world Wikipedia usage. While our tasks are motivated by plausible scenarios, we lack empirical evidence that editors systematically use LLMs in the ways we design them. Nonetheless, the findings of Ford et al. (2023) provide the most systematic basis for aligning our benchmark with real-world editorial contexts.

NPOV Detection To identify the most effective prompting technique for TST, we train four style classifiers per language-level setting (see Appendix Table 9). However, our classifiers for Vietnamese and English at the paragraph level achieve accuracy only slightly above random chance, which might compromise the prompt evaluation in Section 4.3. Despite extensive fine-tuning across model types, data, and hyperparameters, performance remains limited. For both subsets, we report the most conservative results to ensure that, even if classifier performance is poor, the precision of NPOV-related revisions is maximised (see Appendix B.3 for details). We acknowledge that NPOV detection on Vietnamese and English paragraph-level data is intrinsically challenging.

Text Length When comparing detection results between sentence- and paragraph-level TST, we find that text length significantly affects performance. While we stratify samples by tertiles to control for length, we do not further analyse detection performance based on length, instead reporting average metrics. Given its impact, we plan to investigate text-length heterogeneity in future work.

Generalisability Although we aim to cover a broad range of detectors, generators, and languages, our conclusions are limited to the evaluated settings. Due to the rapid pace of AI research, our configurations may quickly become outdated. For example, through advances in LLMs or MGT detectors. To support ongoing progress, we open-source our data and benchmark and plan to maintain the repository to ensure its continued relevance.

Ethics Statement

Our work uses publicly available content from Wikipedia, licensed under CC BY-SA. We include no private or sensitive information, and our experiments pose no risk to Wikipedia editors or the Wikipedias under study. Sensitive data about individual contributors are neither identifiable nor exposed in any way.

We obtain machine-generated data using four LLMs under their respective licences:

- GPT-4-mini: No specific license. OpenAI welcomes research publications.[22]
- Gemini 2.0: Apache 2.0[23]
- QWen 2.0: Apache 2.0[24]
- Mistral: Apache 2.0[25]

This study addresses limitations in prior evaluations of SOTA MGT detectors by systematically assessing their performance in realistic editorial contexts. Our goal is to provide more accurate and practical insights into the feasibility and utility of MGT detection in collaborative knowledge environments such as Wikipedia. We emphasise that our experiments aim to inform the potential role of MGT detectors as automated metrics or as tools to assist users in identifying machine-generated content.

Acknowledgements

This work was supported by the Engineering and Physical Sciences Research Council [grant number Y009800/1], through funding from Responsible AI UK (KP0011), as part of the Participatory Harm Auditing Workbenches and Methodologies (PHAWM) project. Additional support was provided by UK Research and Innovation [grant number EP/S023356/1] through the UKRI Centre for Doctoral Training in Safe and Trusted Artificial Intelligence (www.safeandtrustedai.org).

References

Joshua Ashkinaze, Ruijia Guan, Laura Kurek, Eytan Adar, Ceren Budak, and Eric Gilbert. 2024. Seeing like an ai: How llms apply (and misapply) wikipedia neutrality norms. *Preprint*, arXiv:2407.04183.

Nishant Balepur, Jie Huang, and Kevin Chang. 2023. Expository text generation: Imitate, retrieve, paraphrase. In *Proceedings of the 2023 Conference on Empirical Methods in Natural Language Processing*, pages 11896–11919, Singapore. Association for Computational Linguistics.

Siddhartha Banerjee and Prasenjit Mitra. 2015. WikiKreator: Improving Wikipedia stubs automatically. In *Proceedings of the 53rd Annual Meeting of the Association for Computational Linguistics and the 7th International Joint Conference on Natural Language Processing (Volume 1: Long Papers)*, pages 867–877, Beijing, China. Association for Computational Linguistics.

Guangsheng Bao, Yanbin Zhao, Zhiyang Teng, Linyi Yang, and Yue Zhang. 2023. Fast-detectgpt: Efficient zero-shot detection of machine-generated text via conditional probability curvature. *arXiv preprint arXiv:2310.05130*.

[22]https://openai.com/policies/sharing-publication-policy/

[23]https://github.com/google-gemini

[24]https://github.com/QwenLM/Qwen2.5

[25]https://mistral.ai/news/announcing-mistral-7b

Creston Brooks, Samuel Eggert, and Denis Peskoff. 2024. The rise of ai-generated content in wikipedia. *Preprint*, arXiv:2410.08044.

Tom B. Brown, Benjamin Mann, Nick Ryder, Melanie Subbiah, Jared Kaplan, Prafulla Dhariwal, Arvind Neelakantan, Pranav Shyam, Girish Sastry, Amanda Askell, Sandhini Agarwal, Ariel Herbert-Voss, Gretchen Krueger, Tom Henighan, Rewon Child, Aditya Ramesh, Daniel M. Ziegler, Jeffrey Wu, Clemens Winter, and 12 others. 2020. Language models are few-shot learners. *Preprint*, arXiv:2005.14165.

Silvia Casola, Alberto Lavelli, and 1 others. 2021. Wits: Wikipedia for italian text summarization. In *CLiC-it*.

Arman Cohan, Franck Dernoncourt, Doo Soon Kim, Trung Bui, Seokhwan Kim, Walter Chang, and Nazli Goharian. 2018. A discourse-aware attention model for abstractive summarization of long documents. *arXiv preprint arXiv:1804.05685*.

Alexis Conneau, Kartikay Khandelwal, Naman Goyal, Vishrav Chaudhary, Guillaume Wenzek, Francisco Guzmán, Edouard Grave, Myle Ott, Luke Zettlemoyer, and Veselin Stoyanov. 2020. Unsupervised cross-lingual representation learning at scale. *Preprint*, arXiv:1911.02116.

Selena Deckelmann. 2023. Wikipedia's value in the age of generative ai.

Jacob Devlin, Ming-Wei Chang, Kenton Lee, and Kristina Toutanova. 2019. Bert: Pre-training of deep bidirectional transformers for language understanding. *Preprint*, arXiv:1810.04805.

Jane Dwivedi-Yu, Timo Schick, Zhengbao Jiang, Maria Lomeli, Patrick Lewis, Gautier Izacard, Edouard Grave, Sebastian Riedel, and Fabio Petroni. 2022. Editeval: An instruction-based benchmark for text improvements. *arXiv preprint arXiv:2209.13331*.

Alexander R. Fabbri, Chien-Sheng Wu, Wenhao Liu, and Caiming Xiong. 2022. Qafacteval: Improved qa-based factual consistency evaluation for summarization. *Preprint*, arXiv:2112.08542.

Angela Fan and Claire Gardent. 2022. Generating biographies on Wikipedia: The impact of gender bias on the retrieval-based generation of women biographies. In *Proceedings of the 60th Annual Meeting of the Association for Computational Linguistics (Volume 1: Long Papers)*, pages 8561–8576, Dublin, Ireland. Association for Computational Linguistics.

Heather Ford, Michael Davis, and Timothy Koskie. 2023. Implications of chatgpt for knowledge integrity on wikipedia. Accessed: 2025-04-06.

Isabel O. Gallegos, Ryan A. Rossi, Joe Barrow, Md Mehrab Tanjim, Sungchul Kim, Franck Dernoncourt, Tong Yu, Ruiyi Zhang, and Nesreen K. Ahmed. 2024. Bias and fairness in large language models: A survey. *Preprint*, arXiv:2309.00770.

Shen Gao, Xiuying Chen, Chang Liu, Dongyan Zhao, and Rui Yan. 2021. Biogen: Generating biography summary under table guidance on wikipedia. In *Findings of the Association for Computational Linguistics: ACL-IJCNLP 2021*, pages 4752–4757.

Yunfan Gao, Yun Xiong, Xinyu Gao, Kangxiang Jia, Jinliu Pan, Yuxi Bi, Yi Dai, Jiawei Sun, Meng Wang, and Haofen Wang. 2024. Retrieval-augmented generation for large language models: A survey. *Preprint*, arXiv:2312.10997.

Demian Gholipour Ghalandari, Chris Hokamp, Nghia The Pham, John Glover, and Georgiana Ifrim. 2020. A large-scale multi-document summarization dataset from the wikipedia current events portal. *Preprint*, arXiv:2005.10070.

Tanya Goyal, Junyi Jessy Li, and Greg Durrett. 2022. News summarization and evaluation in the era of gpt-3. *arXiv preprint arXiv:2209.12356*.

Max Grusky, Mor Naaman, and Yoav Artzi. 2018. Newsroom: A dataset of 1.3 million summaries with diverse extractive strategies. In *Proceedings of the 2018 Conference of the North American Chapter of the Association for Computational Linguistics: Human Language Technologies, Volume 1 (Long Papers)*, pages 708–719, New Orleans, Louisiana. Association for Computational Linguistics.

Biyang Guo, Xin Zhang, Ziyuan Wang, Minqi Jiang, Jinran Nie, Yuxuan Ding, Jianwei Yue, and Yupeng Wu. 2023. How close is chatgpt to human experts? comparison corpus, evaluation, and detection. *Preprint*, arXiv:2301.07597.

Abhimanyu Hans, Avi Schwarzschild, Valeriia Cherepanova, Hamid Kazemi, Aniruddha Saha, Micah Goldblum, Jonas Geiping, and Tom Goldstein. 2024. Spotting llms with binoculars: Zero-shot detection of machine-generated text. *arXiv preprint arXiv:2401.12070*.

Hiroaki Hayashi, Prashant Budania, Peng Wang, Chris Ackerson, Raj Neervannan, and Graham Neubig. 2021. Wikiasp: A dataset for multi-domain aspect-based summarization. *Transactions of the Association for Computational Linguistics*, 9:211–225.

Pengcheng He, Jianfeng Gao, and Weizhu Chen. 2023. Debertav3: Improving deberta using electra-style pre-training with gradient-disentangled embedding sharing. *Preprint*, arXiv:2111.09543.

Xinlei He, Xinyue Shen, Zeyuan Chen, Michael Backes, and Yang Zhang. 2024. Mgtbench: Benchmarking machine-generated text detection. In *Proceedings of the 2024 on ACM SIGSAC Conference on Computer and Communications Security*, pages 2251–2265.

Lei Huang, Weijiang Yu, Weitao Ma, Weihong Zhong, Zhangyin Feng, Haotian Wang, Qianglong Chen, Weihua Peng, Xiaocheng Feng, Bing Qin, and 1 others. 2025a. A survey on hallucination in large language models: Principles, taxonomy, challenges, and open questions. *ACM Transactions on Information Systems*, 43(2):1–55.

Siming Huang, Yuliang Xu, Mingmeng Geng, Yao Wan, and Dongping Chen. 2025b. Wikipedia in the era of llms: Evolution and risks. *arXiv preprint arXiv:2503.02879*.

Wenxiang Jiao, Wenxuan Wang, Jen-tse Huang, Xing Wang, Shuming Shi, and Zhaopeng Tu. 2023. Is chatgpt a good translator? yes with gpt-4 as the engine. *arXiv preprint arXiv:2301.08745*.

Faisal Ladhak, Esin Durmus, Claire Cardie, and Kathleen McKeown. 2020. WikiLingua: A new benchmark dataset for cross-lingual abstractive summarization. In *Findings of the Association for Computational Linguistics: EMNLP 2020*, pages 4034–4048, Online. Association for Computational Linguistics.

Yafu Li, Qintong Li, Leyang Cui, Wei Bi, Zhilin Wang, Longyue Wang, Linyi Yang, Shuming Shi, and Yue Zhang. 2023. Mage: Machine-generated text detection in the wild. *arXiv preprint arXiv:2305.13242*.

Chin-Yew Lin. 2004. Rouge: A package for automatic evaluation of summaries. In *Text summarization branches out*, pages 74–81.

Peter J Liu, Mohammad Saleh, Etienne Pot, Ben Goodrich, Ryan Sepassi, Lukasz Kaiser, and Noam Shazeer. 2018. Generating wikipedia by summarizing long sequences. *arXiv preprint arXiv:1801.10198*.

Yinhan Liu, Myle Ott, Naman Goyal, Jingfei Du, Mandar Joshi, Danqi Chen, Omer Levy, Mike Lewis, Luke Zettlemoyer, and Veselin Stoyanov. 2019. Roberta: A robustly optimized bert pretraining approach. *Preprint*, arXiv:1907.11692.

Shayne Longpre, Gregory Yauney, Emily Reif, Katherine Lee, Adam Roberts, Barret Zoph, Denny Zhou, Jason Wei, Kevin Robinson, David Mimno, and Daphne Ippolito. 2023. A pretrainer's guide to training data: Measuring the effects of data age, domain coverage, quality, toxicity. *Preprint*, arXiv:2305.13169.

Dominik Macko, Robert Moro, Adaku Uchendu, Jason Samuel Lucas, Michiharu Yamashita, Matúš Pikuliak, Ivan Srba, Thai Le, Dongwon Lee, Jakub Simko, and 1 others. 2023. Multitude: Large-scale multilingual machine-generated text detection benchmark. *arXiv preprint arXiv:2310.13606*.

Eric Mitchell, Yoonho Lee, Alexander Khazatsky, Christopher D Manning, and Chelsea Finn. 2023. Detectgpt: Zero-shot machine-generated text detection using probability curvature (2023). *arXiv preprint arXiv:2301.11305*.

Ramesh Nallapati, Bowen Zhou, Caglar Gulcehre, Bing Xiang, and 1 others. 2016. Abstractive text summarization using sequence-to-sequence rnns and beyond. *arXiv preprint arXiv:1602.06023*.

OpenAI, Josh Achiam, Steven Adler, Sandhini Agarwal, Lama Ahmad, Ilge Akkaya, Florencia Leoni Aleman, Diogo Almeida, Janko Altenschmidt, Sam Altman, Shyamal Anadkat, Red Avila, Igor Babuschkin, Suchir Balaji, Valerie Balcom, Paul Baltescu, Haiming Bao, Mohammad Bavarian, Jeff Belgum, and 262 others. 2024. Gpt-4 technical report. *Preprint*, arXiv:2303.08774.

Long Ouyang, Jeff Wu, Xu Jiang, Diogo Almeida, Carroll L. Wainwright, Pamela Mishkin, Chong Zhang, Sandhini Agarwal, Katarina Slama, Alex Ray, John Schulman, Jacob Hilton, Fraser Kelton, Luke Miller, Maddie Simens, Amanda Askell, Peter Welinder, Paul Christiano, Jan Leike, and Ryan Lowe. 2022. Training language models to follow instructions with human feedback. *Preprint*, arXiv:2203.02155.

Kishore Papineni, Salim Roukos, Todd Ward, and Wei-Jing Zhu. 2002. Bleu: a method for automatic evaluation of machine translation. In *Proceedings of the 40th annual meeting of the Association for Computational Linguistics*, pages 311–318.

Laura Perez-Beltrachini and Mirella Lapata. 2022. Models and datasets for cross-lingual summarisation. *arXiv preprint arXiv:2202.09583*.

Reid Pryzant, Richard Diehl Martinez, Nathan Dass, Sadao Kurohashi, Dan Jurafsky, and Diyi Yang. 2020. Automatically neutralizing subjective bias in text. In *Proceedings of the aaai conference on artificial intelligence*, volume 34, pages 480–489.

Xiao Pu, Mingqi Gao, and Xiaojun Wan. 2023. Summarization is (almost) dead. *arXiv preprint arXiv:2309.09558*.

Hongjing Qian, Yutao Zhu, Zhicheng Dou, Haoqi Gu, Xinyu Zhang, Zheng Liu, Ruofei Lai, Zhao Cao, Jian-Yun Nie, and Ji-Rong Wen. 2023. Webbrain: Learning to generate factually correct articles for queries by grounding on large web corpus. *Preprint*, arXiv:2304.04358.

Pranav Rajpurkar, Jian Zhang, Konstantin Lopyrev, and Percy Liang. 2016. Squad: 100,000+ questions for machine comprehension of text. *Preprint*, arXiv:1606.05250.

Emily Reif, Daphne Ippolito, Ann Yuan, Andy Coenen, Chris Callison-Burch, and Jason Wei. 2021. A recipe for arbitrary text style transfer with large language models. *arXiv preprint arXiv:2109.03910*.

Marija Sakota, Maxime Peyrard, and Robert West. 2023. Descartes: Generating short descriptions of wikipedia articles. In *Proceedings of the ACM Web Conference 2023*, WWW '23, page 1446–1456, New York, NY, USA. Association for Computing Machinery.

K. Salas-Jimenez, Francisco Fernando Lopez-Ponce, Sergio-Luis Ojeda-Trueba, and Gemma Bel-Enguix. 2024. WikiBias as an extrapolation corpus for bias detection. In *Proceedings of the First Workshop on Advancing Natural Language Processing for Wikipedia*, pages 46–52, Miami, Florida, USA. Association for Computational Linguistics.

Christina Sauper and Regina Barzilay. 2009. Automatically generating Wikipedia articles: A structure-aware approach. In *Proceedings of the Joint Conference of the 47th Annual Meeting of the ACL and the 4th International Joint Conference on Natural Language Processing of the AFNLP*, pages 208–216, Suntec, Singapore. Association for Computational Linguistics.

Yijia Shao, Yucheng Jiang, Theodore A. Kanell, Peter Xu, Omar Khattab, and Monica S. Lam. 2024. Assisting in writing wikipedia-like articles from scratch with large language models. *Preprint*, arXiv:2402.14207.

Ilia Shumailov, Zakhar Shumaylov, Yiren Zhao, Nicolas Papernot, Ross Anderson, and Yarin Gal. 2024. Ai models collapse when trained on recursively generated data. *Nature*, 631(8022):755–759.

Jinyan Su, Terry Yue Zhuo, Di Wang, and Preslav Nakov. 2023. Detectllm: Leveraging log rank information for zero-shot detection of machine-generated text. *arXiv preprint arXiv:2306.05540*.

Zhen Tao, Zhiyu Li, Dinghao Xi, and Wei Xu. 2024. Cudrt: Benchmarking the detection of human vs. large language models generated texts. *arXiv preprint arXiv:2406.09056*.

Adaku Uchendu, Zeyu Ma, Thai Le, Rui Zhang, and Dongwon Lee. 2021. TURINGBENCH: A benchmark environment for Turing test in the age of neural text generation. In *Findings of the Association for Computational Linguistics: EMNLP 2021*, Punta Cana, Dominican Republic. Association for Computational Linguistics.

Yuxia Wang, Jonibek Mansurov, Petar Ivanov, Jinyan Su, Artem Shelmanov, Akim Tsvigun, Osama Mohanned Afzal, Tarek Mahmoud, Giovanni Puccetti, Thomas Arnold, and 1 others. 2024a. M4gt-bench: Evaluation benchmark for black-box machine-generated text detection. *arXiv preprint arXiv:2402.11175*.

Yuxia Wang, Jonibek Mansurov, Petar Ivanov, Jinyan Su, Artem Shelmanov, Akim Tsvigun, Osama Mohammed Afzal, Tarek Mahmoud, Giovanni Puccetti, Thomas Arnold, Alham Aji, Nizar Habash, Iryna Gurevych, and Preslav Nakov. 2024b. M4GT-bench: Evaluation benchmark for black-box machine-generated text detection. In *Proceedings of the 62nd Annual Meeting of the Association for Computational Linguistics (Volume 1: Long Papers)*, Bangkok, Thailand. Association for Computational Linguistics.

Yuxia Wang, Jonibek Mansurov, Petar Ivanov, Jinyan Su, Artem Shelmanov, Akim Tsvigun, Chenxi Whitehouse, Osama Mohammed Afzal, Tarek Mahmoud, Toru Sasaki, and 1 others. 2023. M4: Multi-generator, multi-domain, and multi-lingual black-box machine-generated text detection. *arXiv preprint arXiv:2305.14902*.

Junchao Wu, Runzhe Zhan, Derek Wong, Shu Yang, Xinyi Yang, Yulin Yuan, and Lidia Chao. 2024. Detectrl: Benchmarking llm-generated text detection in real-world scenarios. *Advances in Neural Information Processing Systems*, 37:100369–100401.

Junchao Wu, Runzhe Zhan, Derek F. Wong, Shu Yang, Xuebo Liu, Lidia S. Chao, and Min Zhang. 2025. Who wrote this? the key to zero-shot llm-generated text detection is gecscore. *Preprint*, arXiv:2405.04286.

Jianhao Yan, Pingchuan Yan, Yulong Chen, Judy Li, Xianchao Zhu, and Yue Zhang. 2024. Gpt-4 vs. human translators: A comprehensive evaluation of translation quality across languages, domains, and expertise levels. *arXiv preprint arXiv:2407.03658*.

Xianjun Yang, Liangming Pan, Xuandong Zhao, Haifeng Chen, Linda Petzold, William Yang Wang, and Wei Cheng. 2023. A survey on detection of llms-generated content. *arXiv preprint arXiv:2310.15654*.

Jiebin Zhang, Eugene J. Yu, Qinyu Chen, Chenhao Xiong, Dawei Zhu, Han Qian, Mingbo Song, Weimin Xiong, Xiaoguang Li, Qun Liu, and Sujian Li. 2025. WIKIGENBENCH:exploring full-length Wikipedia generation under real-world scenario. In *Proceedings of the 31st International Conference on Computational Linguistics*, pages 5191–5210, Abu Dhabi, UAE. Association for Computational Linguistics.

Tianyi Zhang, Varsha Kishore, Felix Wu, Kilian Q Weinberger, and Yoav Artzi. 2019. Bertscore: Evaluating text generation with bert. *arXiv preprint arXiv:1904.09675*.

Tianyi Zhang, Faisal Ladhak, Esin Durmus, Percy Liang, Kathleen McKeown, and Tatsunori B. Hashimoto. 2023. Benchmarking large language models for news summarization. *Preprint*, arXiv:2301.13848.

Tianyi Zhang, Faisal Ladhak, Esin Durmus, Percy Liang, Kathleen McKeown, and Tatsunori B Hashimoto. 2024. Benchmarking large language models for news summarization. *Transactions of the Association for Computational Linguistics*, 12:39–57.

Jingyi Zheng, Junfeng Wang, Zhen Sun, Wenhan Dong, Yule Liu, and Xinlei He. 2025. Th-bench: Evaluating evading attacks via humanizing ai text on machine-generated text detectors. *arXiv preprint arXiv:2503.08708*.

Yang Zhong, Jingfeng Yang, Wei Xu, and Diyi Yang. 2021. WIKIBIAS: Detecting multi-span subjective biases in language. In *Findings of the Association for Computational Linguistics: EMNLP 2021*, pages 1799–1814, Punta Cana, Dominican Republic. Association for Computational Linguistics.

Biru Zhu, Lifan Yuan, Ganqu Cui, Yangyi Chen, Chong Fu, Bingxiang He, Yangdong Deng, Zhiyuan Liu, Maosong Sun, and Ming Gu. 2023a. Beat llms at their own game: Zero-shot llm-generated text detection via querying chatgpt. In *Proceedings of the 2023 Conference on Empirical Methods in Natural Language Processing*, pages 7470–7483.

Wenhao Zhu, Hongyi Liu, Qingxiu Dong, Jingjing Xu, Shujian Huang, Lingpeng Kong, Jiajun Chen, and Lei Li. 2023b. Multilingual machine translation with large language models: Empirical results and analysis. *arXiv preprint arXiv:2304.04675*.

A Data Construction

We download the meta stub history WikiDumps[26] for all three languages, which serve as the foundational datasets for both **WikiPS** and the **mWNC**. For both datasets, we consider only the most recent instances—revisions for mWNC and article versions for WikiPS—that occurred prior to the public release of ChatGPT on 30 November 2022. This filtering step ensures that our data is not contaminated by MGT.

A.1 WikiPS

We begin by retrieving the latest revision IDs for all *articles* (excluding discussion pages and other non-content pages) in each target language. We then randomly sample and crawl these articles by querying the MediaWiki Action API[27] until we collect 100,000 non-stub Wikipedia articles in HTML format per language. Rather than concentrating on a set of topics, we rely on a large enough random sample to provide a representative snapshot of each Wikipedia. We also rely on HTML representations, as parsing raw MediaWiki markup often leads to errors and occasional information loss (e.g., incomplete internal links).

We filter out articles lacking essential structural elements, such as a title, lead section, content sections, or references, as well as list-based articles. From the remaining articles, we use `BeautifulSoup` to pre-process, clean, and parse the HTML and extract the following components: the lead section, infobox (if available), paragraphs with their section headers (excluding sections such as "See also", "External links", etc.), and reference lists. This process yields article-level corpora of 67,267 articles in English, 56,538 in Portuguese, and 60,884 in Vietnamese.

Paragraphs To construct our paragraph-level dataset, we randomly sample 20,000 articles per language. We then define a paragraph as a block of text containing at least three sentences and a minimum of 20 characters. For each paragraph, we collect metadata including its position within the article and any associated external references. We further refine the dataset by removing paragraphs without any references and those whose token counts fall outside two standard deviations from the mean token count of the corpus. Based on the filtered corpus, we compute tertiles for each paragraph and assign each to its corresponding range (EN $(83.0, 120.0)$; PT $(88.0, 128.0)$; VI $(108.0, 160.0)$). For the Paragraph Writing task, we only consider the first paragraph following a section or subsection. The resulting raw paragraph-level corpora consist of 96,860 paragraphs in English, 72,965 in Portuguese, and 98,315 in Vietnamese.

Summaries To construct our summarisation dataset, we extract the lead section, infobox, and article body from the processed text corpora for each article. For the English and Portuguese corpora, we exclude lead sections with fewer than 10 tokens or with token lengths exceeding two standard deviations above the token mean. Similarly, we discard article bodies with fewer than 100 tokens or more than two standard deviations above the mean token count. For the Vietnamese corpus, whose article bodies are considerably longer (see Table 7), we set an upper limit of either 2,900 tokens or two standard deviations above the mean to mitigate context length constraints during model processing. As we treat each component as text input, we apply minimal markdown-like formatting to both the infobox and article body, such as rendering headers in bold. The resulting summarisation corpora consist of 53,203 lead–article pairs in English, 36,075 in Portuguese, and 45,500 in Vietnamese.

Table 7 compares our raw summarisation datasets to three commonly used benchmarks from different domains: WikiLingua (Ladhak et al., 2020) for Wikimedia content, CNN/DM (Nallapati et al., 2016) for news, and arXiv (Cohan et al., 2018) for academic writing.

On average, our summaries are considerably longer than those in WikiLingua and CNN/DM, but shorter than arXiv abstracts. The average body length in our datasets is comparable to CNN/DM but significantly shorter than arXiv. Despite this, our datasets exhibit higher ROUGE-1 and ROUGE-2 scores, indicating improved content overlap. We also observe lower compression rates (Grusky et al., 2018), meaning our summaries are proportionally longer relative to article bodies. Furthermore, our datasets show consistently higher percentages of novel unigrams, bigrams, and trigrams, suggesting a greater degree of abstractiveness.

To address the concern that a higher proportion of novel tokens may signal information asymmetry between the lead and the article body, we com-

[26]`https://dumps.wikimedia.org/`

[27]`https://www.mediawiki.org/wiki/API:Main_page`

Corpus	Subset	Level	Language	Corpus N	Processed Corpus N	Eval N	Experiment N	MGT N
extendWNC	Text Style Transfer	Sentences	EN	2,333,143	286,626	270	2,700	10,800
			PT	31,506	7,877	270	2700	10,800
			VI	13,800	1,185	270	1185	4,740
		Paragraphs	EN	4,671	4,671	270	2700	10,800
WikiPS	Paragraph Writing		EN	96,860	96,860	270	2700	10,800
			PT	72,965	72,965	270	2700	10,800
			VI	98,315	98,315	270	2700	10,800
	Summarisation		EN	67,267	53,203	270	2700	10,800
			PT	56,538	36,075	270	2700	10,800
			VI	60,884	45,500	270	2700	10,800
Total						**2,700**	**25,485**	**101,940**

Table 6: WETBench Dataset Statistics. Corpus N denotes the raw number of observations; Processed N denotes the number of observations after processing; Experiment N denotes the number of human-written texts; and MGT N denotes the total number of machine-generated texts.

Metric/Corpus	WikiLingua	CNN/DM	arXiv	WikiSums EN	WikiSums PT	WikiSums VI
Size	142,346	311,971	215,913	67,267	56,538	60,884
Summary Length	32 (19)	51 (21)	272 (572)	83 (78)	87 (95)	135 (148)
Body Length	379 (224)	690 (337)	6029 (4570)	667 (1027)	587 (1121)	940 (1800)
Infobox Length	-	-	-	61 (60)	62 (40)	95 (78)
ROUGE-1	0.13	0.14	0.07	0.17	0.18	0.30
ROUGE-2	0.05	0.08	0.04	0.06	0.06	0.16
Compression Rate	14.12	14.66	39.78	10.30	7.80	8.56
Novel Unigram %	0.38	0.20	0.15	0.53	0.62	0.49
Novel Bigram %	0.78	0.60	0.45	0.83	0.88	0.80
Novel Trigram %	0.93	0.77	0.69	0.93	0.95	0.91
Entity Sample Size	20,000	20,000	20,000	20,000	20,000	20,000
Entity F1-Score	0.06	0.21	0.04	0.14	0.17	0.13

Table 7: Summarisation Corpora Comparison. Numbers in parentheses report standard deviation.

pute entity overlap F1-scores on a 20,000-example subset of each dataset. Our results show higher entity F1-scores compared to WikiLingua, CNN/DM, and arXiv, indicating that our datasets maintain a comparable or better level of factual consistency.

Among the Wikipedias, the Vietnamese edition features leads, infoboxes, and article bodies that are approximately 30% longer than their English and Portuguese counterparts. Despite higher ROUGE scores, the comparable share of novel n-grams in Vietnamese indicates a slightly lower level of abstractiveness relative to the other language versions.

A.2 mWNC

We largely follow the procedure of Pryzant et al. (2020), with modifications to accommodate larger multilingual datasets. From each Wikidump, we extract all NPOV-related revisions made prior to the release of ChatGPT. We expand the set of NPOV-related keywords (e.g., NPOV, POV, neutral, etc.) for each Wikipedia edition based on its respective NPOV policy page.[28] This yields 2,333,143 relevant revisions for English, 31,506 for Portuguese, and 13,800 for Vietnamese.

We retrieve the corresponding diffs[29] using the MediaWiki API,[30] which we extensively clean and pre-process. To match pre- and post-neutralisation sentence pairs within each edit chunk, we first discard all unedited sentences and then apply pairwise BLEU scoring to identify the highest-scoring sentence pairs. For details on chunk and sentence filtering, we refer to Pryzant et al. (2020).

Our main modifications include: (*1*) retaining reverts, and (*2*) for Vietnamese only, relaxing the Levenshtein distance threshold to <3 and allowing up to two edit chunk pairs and multiple sentence-level matches. This adjustment addresses the comparatively low number of NPOV-related edits in Vietnamese, which would otherwise yield only a few hundred usable instances.

These modifications result in 286,626 sentence pairs for English, 7,877 for Portuguese, and 1,185 for Vietnamese. While we could further increase N for Vietnamese by loosening the filtering criteria, we find that this introduces noise and does not improve the performance of the downstream style classifier. We therefore prioritise a smaller, higher-precision dataset (see also Appendix B.3).

Due to the stark disparity in data size, we obtain paragraph-level data only for English. For this, we construct a dataset that, like the Vietnamese setup, allows multiple edit chunk and sentence-level matches. We define a paragraph-level pair as one in which at least one addition or deletion occurs in each of three adjacent sentences. This yields a dataset of 4,671 paragraph pairs.

B Task Design Details

For brevity, we present prompts in English only.

[28] English: Neutral point of view; Portuguese: Princípio da imparcialidade; Vietnamese: Thái đ trung lp

[29] `https://en.wikipedia.org/wiki/Help:Diff`

[30] 3027

B.1 Paragraph Writing

B.1.1 Paragraph Writing Prompts

Minimal

```
Please write the first paragraph for the section
      "{section_title}" in the Wikipedia article
     "{page_title}" using no more than {n_words}
     words. Only return the paragraph.
```

Content Prompts

```
Please write the first paragraph for the section
      "{section_title}" in the Wikipedia article
     "{page_title}".

Address the following key points in your
     response:
{content_prompts}

Use no more than {n_words} words. Only return
     the paragraph.
```

RAG

```
Use the following context to ensure factual
     accuracy when writing:
{context}

--

Please write the first paragraph for the section
      "{section_title}" in the Wikipedia article
     "{page_title}".

Address the following key points in your
     response:
{content_prompts}

Use the context above to inform your response,
     in addition to any relevant knowledge you
     have. Use no more than {n_words} words. Only
      return the paragraph in {language}.
```

B.1.2 Content Prompts

We model editors' LLM-assisted content generation through Content Prompts. For instance, an editor aiming to expand a Wikipedia article might prompt a model to generate a paragraph in response to factual questions about a specific topic (e.g., "What are London's most notable modern buildings?" or "What is London's tallest skyscraper?"), within a given section (e.g., Architecture). For each human-written paragraph in our dataset, we prompt GPT-4o (OpenAI et al., 2024) to generate a minimum of five content prompts for low-tertile paragraphs, and eight for medium- and high-tertile paragraphs. Although this method does not exhaustively cover all factual content from the HWT, it substantially improves the alignment of factual information between HWT and MGT.

B.1.3 Naive RAG

We implement a web-based Naive RAG setup to reflect an editing scenario in which an editor, in addition to providing task instructions and content prompts, also supplies relevant context to minimise factual inaccuracies. Our RAG pipeline follows the indexing, retrieval, and generation modules of the Naive variant (Gao et al., 2024), with two key modifications: we prepend the pipeline with Content Prompts and Web Search modules.

Content Prompts and Web Search For each paragraph, we generate diverse content prompts as described above. We use each content prompt to query the Google Custom Search API,[31] retrieving the top 10 most relevant URLs. From the search results, we exclude the original Wikipedia page (if applicable) as well as any unreliable sources (Shao et al., 2024).

Indexing We download the raw HTML of each scrappable web page and apply a series of preprocessing and cleaning steps. We then split each page into chunks using LangChain's RecursiveCharacterTextSplitter.[32] We compute BGE-M3[33] embeddings for each chunk and store them in a vector database.

Retrieval and Generation We treat each content prompt as a query, compute its embedding, and retrieve the two most similar chunks from the vector database based on cosine similarity. We append these retrieved chunks to the content prompt as context to guide the model's generation.

B.2 Summarisation

B.2.1 Prompts

Minimal

```
Your task is to summarize the below article with
      no more than {n_toks_trgt} words. Article:

"""{src}"""
```

Instruction/Few-Shot

```
Your task is to summarize an article to create a
      Wikipedia lead section.
- In Wikipedia, the lead section is an
     introduction to an article and a summary of
     its most important contents.
```

[31] https://developers.google.com/custom-search/v1/overview

[32] LangChain RecursiveCharacterTextSplitter documentation

[33] https://huggingface.co/BAAI/bge-m3

```
- Apart from basic facts, significant
    information should not appear in the lead if
     it is not covered in the remainder of the
    article.

Generate the lead for the article titled "{
    page_title}" using the article's body above
    with no more than {n_toks_trgt} words.
    Article:

"""{src}"""
```

B.3 TST

B.3.1 Prompts

Minimal

```
Please make this sentence/paragraph more neutral.
     **Make as few changes as possible and use
    no more than {trgt_n_words} words for the
    neutralised sentence/paragraph.** Sentence/
    Paragraph:

"""{src}"""
```

Instruction/Few-Shot

```
Please edit this biased Wikipedia sentence/
    paragraph to make it more neutral, aligning
    with Wikipedia's neutral point of view
    policy:

Achieving what the Wikipedia community
    understands as neutrality means carefully
    and critically analyzing a variety of
    reliable sources and then attempting to
    convey to the reader the information
    contained in them fairly, proportionately,
    and as far as possible without editorial
    bias. Wikipedia aims to describe disputes,
    but not engage in them. The aim is to inform
    , not influence. Editors, while naturally
    having their own points of view, should
    strive in good faith to provide complete
    information and not to promote one
    particular point of view over another. The
    neutral point of view does not mean the
    exclusion of certain points of view; rather,
     it means including all verifiable points of
     view which have sufficient due weight.
    Observe the following principles to help
    achieve the level of neutrality that is
    appropriate for an encyclopedia:

- Avoid stating opinions as facts.
- Avoid stating seriously contested assertions
    as facts.
- Avoid stating facts as opinions.
- Prefer nonjudgmental language.
- Do not editorialize.
- Indicate the relative prominence of opposing
    views.

**Make as few changes as possible and use no
    more than {trgt_n_words} words for the
    neutralised sentence/paragraph.** Output
    only the neutralized sentence/paragraph.
    Sentence/Paragraph:

"""{src}"""
```

B.3.2 Style Classifiers

We fine-tune four style classifiers: one for each language at the sentence level, and an additional classifier for English at the paragraph level. The hyperparameter settings are provided in Table 8.

Language/Level	Models	Learning Rate	Batch Sizes	Epochs	Weight Decay
EN/Sent.	roberta-base	1e-6	32	15	0.01
PT/Sent.	xlm-roberta-base, mBERT	5e-5, 1e-5, 5e-6	16, 32	2, 5, 8	0, 0.01
VI/Sent.	xlm-roberta-base, mBERT	5e-5, 1e-5, 5e-6, 1e-6	16, 32	2, 4, 6	0, 0.01
EN/Para.	roberta-base	5e-5, 1e-6, 5e-6	16, 32	3, 6, 9	0, 0.01

Table 8: Style Classifier Hyperparameter Settings.

For English, we adopt the hyperparameters from the best-performing neutrality classifier available on Hugging Face.[34] As the English data contain nearly a quarter of a million sentence pairs, we fine-tune on a smaller subset of the most recent 150k pairs, specifically filtered to include the keyword *NPOV* in the revision content, in order to further enhance precision. For Portuguese, we apply commonly used hyperparameter values, while for Vietnamese and English paragraphs, we extend the search space, as initial experiments yielded low detection performance.

Level	Language	Pairs	Test Accuracy
Sentences	English	300,000	73%
	Portuguese	5738	63%
	Vietnamese	2370	58%
Paragraphs	English	9342	58%

Table 9: Style Transfer Classifier Performance. Pairs denote biased and neutralised samples.

Table 9 reports the style classifier hyperparameter fine-tuning results. While fine-tuned models for English and Portuguese sentences yield satisfactory results, style accuracy for English paragraphs and Vietnamese sentences is low. In the following, we provide a qualitative analysis of both subsets and explain how we address these low performances.

Low Style Classifier Performance Analysis Table 10 presents two representative examples of NPOV revisions from each subset. The first example in each case illustrates a clear NPOV violation. For instance, the phrase "considered the

[34]https://huggingface.co/cffl/bert-base-styleclassification-subjective-neutral

best footballer" in Vietnamese and "not as strong" in English are both subjective. However, as illustrated with the second examples, NPOV filtering also captures revisions related to political or historical content, which often rely on (subjectively) factual corrections rather than systematic semantic cues.

Subset	Biased Examples
Vietnamese	***Đc coi là cu th xut sc nht th gii và là cu th vĩ đi nht mi thi đi (Greatest of All Time - GOAT)****, Ronaldo là ch nhân ca 5 Qu bóng vàng châu Âu vào các năm 2008, 2013, 2014, 2016, 2017 và cũng là ch nhân 4 Chic giày vàng châu Âu, c hai đu là k lc ca mt cu th châu Âu cùng nhiu danh hiu cao quý khác.* (EN: Considered the best football player in the world and the greatest of all time (GOAT), Ronaldo has won 5 Ballon d'Or awards in the years 2008, 2013, 2014, 2016, and 2017, as well as 4 European Golden Shoes—both records for a European player—along with many other prestigious titles.)
	Ông tng phc v Lý Hoài Tiên, tng di quyn ***nghch tc*** *S T Minh ca Ngy Yên.* (EN: He once served Lý Hoài Tiên, a general under the command of the rebel S T Minh of Ngy Yên.)
English Paragraphs	*He is* ***not as strong****, although still an exceptional warrior. Agamemnon clearly has a stubborn streak that* ***one can argue makes him even more arrogant*** *than Achilles. Although he takes few risks in battle, Agamemnon* ***still accomplishes great progress*** *for the Greeks.*
	The population of Bangladesh ranks seventh in the world, but its area of approximately is ranked ***ninety-fourth****, making it one of the most densely populated countries in the world, or the most densely populated country if small island nations and city-states are not included. It is the third-largest Muslim-majority nation,* ***but*** *has a smaller Muslim population than the Muslim minority in India. Geographically* ***dominated*** *by the fertile Ganges-Brahmaputra Delta, the country has annual monsoon floods, and cyclones are frequent.*

Table 10: NPOV Revision Examples. Parentheses contain English translations. Highlighted words indicate words that were edited.

As we observed this pattern consistently across both subsets, we conducted additional data processing and hyperparameter tuning for the classifiers. We explored several strategies, including: (1) extending the list of NPOV-related keywords, (2) allowing multiple edit chunks per revision, (3) permitting multi-sentence edits within a single chunk, and (4) expanding the range of hyperparameter settings and model types. However, none of these approaches significantly improved style classifier performance.

Therefore, we selected the configuration that yielded the highest precision, adopting a conservative approach to extract NPOV-relevant revision pairs. Despite the relatively low classifier accuracy, we are confident that our dataset includes a high proportion of true positives.

C Detector Details and Implementations

We follow the taxonomy for detecting MGT proposed by (Yang et al., 2023), which categorises detectors into three types: 1) zero-shot, 2) training-based, and 3) watermarking, although we exclude the latter from our experiments. The taxonomy further divides zero-shot methods into white-box and black-box, depending on whether the detector has access to the generator's logits or other model internals. For all detectors, when the original baseline LLM does not support one of our languages, we replace it with a multilingual model of comparable size. For zero-shot detectors, we use Youden's J statistic to determine the optimal threshold.

Zero-shot White-box

LLR (Su et al., 2023) The Log-Likelihood Log-Rank Ratio (LLR) intuitively leverages the ratio of absolute confidence through log-likelihood to relative confidence through log rank for a given sequence. We implement this detector with Bloom-3B.[35]

Binoculars (Hans et al., 2024) Binoculars introduces a metric based on the ratio of perplexity to cross-perplexity, where the latter measures how surprising the next-token predictions of one model are to another. We implement this detector using Qwen2.5-7B[36] for the observer model and Qwen2.5-7B-Instruct[37] for the performer model.

FastDetectGPT White-Box (Bao et al., 2023) DetectGPT (Mitchell et al., 2023) exploits the observation that MGT tends to be located in regions of negative curvature in the log-probability function, from which a curvature-based detection criterion is defined. FastDetectGPT (WB) is an optimised version of DetectGPT that builds on the *conditional*

[35]https://huggingface.co/bigscience/bloom-3b
[36]https://huggingface.co/Qwen/Qwen2.5-7B
[37]https://huggingface.co/Qwen/Qwen2.5-7B-Instruct

Hyperparameter	Values
Batch Size	16, 32
Learning Rate	1e-5, 5e-6, 1e-6
Epochs	3, 5

Table 11: Hyperparameter settings for supervised-detectors.

probability curvature. We implement the white-box version with Bloom-3B.[35]

Zero-shot Black-box

Revise (Zhu et al., 2023a) Revise builds on the hypothesis that ChatGPT[38] performs fewer revisions when generating MGT, and thus bases its detection criterion on the similarity between the original and revised articles. We implement this detector as in the original paper, using GPT-3.5-turbo.[39]

GECScore (Wu et al., 2025) Grammar Error Correction Score assumes that HWT contain more grammatical errors and calculates a Grammatical Error Correction score. We implement this detector as in the original paper, using GPT-3.5-turbo.[39]

FastDetectGPT Black-Box (Hans et al., 2024) In the black-box version, the scoring model differs from the reference model. We use BLOOM-3B as the reference model and BLOOM-1.7B as the scoring model.

Supervised

XLM-RoBERTa (Conneau et al., 2020): XLM-RoBERTa[40] is the multilingual version of RoBERTa (Liu et al., 2019) for 100 languages. RoBERTa improves upon BERT (Devlin et al., 2019) through longer and more extensive training, as well as dynamic masking.

mDeBERTaV3 mDeBERTaV3[41] is the multilingual version of DeBERTa (He et al., 2023), which enhances BERT and RoBERTa using disentangled attention and an improved masked decoder.

[38] https://openai.com

[39] https://platform.openai.com/docs/models/gpt-3.5-turbo

[40] https://huggingface.co/FacebookAI/xlm-roberta-base

[41] https://huggingface.co/microsoft/mdeberta-v3-base

Both models are fine-tuned per task and language on an 80/10/10 split with the hyperparameter choices displayed in Table 11.

D Additional Results

D.1 Mistral Error Analysis

We observe anomalous evaluation metrics for Vietnamese texts written by Mistral. While both zero-shot detectors achieve random chance accuracy and often zero F1-scores, training-based detectors achieve near-perfect metrics. Upon inspecting the data, we find that Mistral, unlike the other models, fails to follow the instructions in our prompts. Common errors include outputting text mid-sentence or returning English text, despite the final sentences of our prompts emphasising that the response should be in Vietnamese. These flaws explain the strong performance of training-based detectors, as they detect such syntactic imperfections, whereas zero-shot detectors appear unable to identify clear patterns based on model internals or token-level features.

E Paper Checklist

Benefits

Q1 *How does this work support the Wikimedia community?*

A1 We believe our work supports the Wikimedia community in at least two ways. First, we introduce two new text corpora that extend beyond MGT detection and can be leveraged for various AI applications. The mWNC dataset addresses (1) community requests to expand existing resources with additional languages, and (2) high-priority needs identified by workshop organizers for NPOV datasets to train and evaluate models for biased language detection. These data open up several research directions, such as training models to detect bias in longer text sequences and testing their generalisability across varying text lengths. As our style classifier results suggest, NPOV detection in low-resource languages remains challenging, making mWNC a valuable resource for advancing this area of research.

Likewise, with WikiPS, we aim to provide two large-scale subsets of general interest to the research community. The paragraph-level subset, for instance, can be used to build question answering datasets for non-high-resource languages, analogous to SQuAD (Rajpurkar et al., 2016). Our summarisation subset naturally lends itself to improving lead section summarisation models. We highlight the inclusion of infoboxes as a key input feature for lead generation, in line with recent findings that LLM-generated summaries are often on par with—or even preferred over—human-written ones (Goyal et al., 2022; Pu et al., 2023; Zhang et al., 2024).

Second, our benchmark, WETBench, is designed to inform the Wikipedia community about the feasibility and effectiveness of current state-of-the-art detectors in identifying MGT instances on the platform. As outlined in the introduction, there is growing concern about the influx of low-quality, unreliable machine-generated content. Due to limitations in prior evaluations (see Section 1), we hope our work contributes to a better understanding of the capabilities and limitations of current detectors, supporting future research and real-world efforts to identify and manage MGT on Wikipedia.

Q2 What license are you using for your data, code, models? Are they available for community re-use?

A2 We release our datasets, WikiPS and mWNC, which are derived from Wikipedia, under the CC BY-SA 4.0 license. Users of the MGT included in our benchmark must ensure compliance with the respective licenses of each language model (see Ethics Statement). We open-source all code used in our work.

Q3 Did you provide clear descriptions and rationale for any filtering that you applied to your data? For example, did you filter to just one language (e.g., English Wikipedia) or many? Did you filter to any specific geographies or topics?

A3 We provide comprehensive explanations of our dataset construction in Section 3 and Appendix A. Section 3 outlines the high-level construction process and key design choices, while Appendix A offers a detailed walkthrough for readers interested in replicating or closely examining our methodology. For fine-grained construction details, we refer readers to our publicly available codebase.

Risks

Q1 If there are risks from your work, do any of them apply specifically to Wikimedia editors or the projects?

A1 Our research objective is to provide a more accurate assessment of SOTA MGT detectors' performance on task-specific MGT. We acknowledge that our findings could be misinterpreted or misused to claim that SOTA detectors are ineffective at identifying machine-assisted edits. However, the intent of our work is not to undermine the potential of detection methods but to highlight their current limitations in realistic editorial settings.

Q2 Did you name any Wikimedia editors (including username) or provide information exposing an editor's identity?

A2 No. Our data includes only textual information, without any references to individual editors.

Q3 Could your research be used to infer sensitive data about individual editors? If so, please explain further.

A3 No. While our dataset includes revision IDs, it does not contain any additional information that is not already publicly available on Wikipedia.

Proper Noun Diacritization for Arabic Wikipedia: A Benchmark Dataset

Rawan Bondok,[1] Mayar Nassar,[1,2] Salam Khalifa,[1,3] Kurt Micallef,[1,4] Nizar Habash[1]
Computational Approaches to Modeling Language (CAMeL) Lab
[1]New York University Abu Dhabi, [2]Ain Shams University
[3]Stony Brook University, [4]Department of Artificial Intelligence, University of Malta
{rawan.bondok,nizar.habash}@nyu.edu, mayar.nassar@art.asu.edu.eg
salam.khalifa@stonybrook.edu, kurt.micallef@um.edu.mt

Abstract

Proper nouns in Arabic Wikipedia are frequently undiacritized, creating ambiguity in pronunciation and interpretation, especially for transliterated named entities of foreign origin. While transliteration and diacritization have been well-studied separately in Arabic NLP, their intersection remains underexplored. In this paper, we introduce a new manually diacritized dataset of Arabic proper nouns of various origins with their English Wikipedia equivalent glosses, and present the challenges and guidelines we followed to create it. We benchmark GPT-4o on the task of recovering full diacritization given the undiacritized Arabic and English forms, and analyze its performance. Achieving 73% accuracy, our results underscore both the difficulty of the task and the need for improved models and resources. We release our dataset to facilitate further research on Arabic Wikipedia proper noun diacritization.[1]

Figure 1: Four Arabic Wikipedia entries: (a) عمان *ςmAn* 'Oman', (b) عمان *ςmAn* 'Amman', (c) لندن *lndn* 'London', and (d) نخجوان *nxjwAn* 'Nakhchivan'. All titles lack diacritics. Lead sentences do not consistently use diacritics: (a) ***ςumAn***, (b) ***ςam∼aAn***, and (c) ***landan***; but (d) lacks diacritics, allowing multiple readings.

1 Introduction

Arabic Wikipedia, like other language editions, has been a valuable resource for both its readers and NLP research. In this paper, we focus on a particular limitation rooted in Arabic's abjad orthography, where diacritics are typically omitted (Elgamal et al., 2024) except for children's books and religious texts. This omission leads to ambiguity in pronunciation and interpretation, especially for proper nouns. Some Arabic Wikipedia articles address this issue by providing partial or full diacritization in their lead sentences. For instance, عمان *ςmAn*[2] can refer to either عُمَان *ςumaAn* 'Oman' or عَمَّان *ςam∼aAn* 'Amman' depending on the diacritization (Figure 1). But more often than not, these diacritics are missing. In our dataset we found 99.45% of all entries had no diacritics. Our intention is to solve this limitation.

The work presented in this paper lies at the intersection of three commonly but often independently studied Arabic NLP tasks: *transliteration*, *diacritization*, and *lemmatization*.

Transliteration is the mapping of words, primarily proper nouns, from one script to another, usually in the context of machine translation (Beesley, 1997; Benites et al., 2020; Chen et al., 2018). It poses challenges due to misalignments between scripts, differences in representing phonology and

[1]https://github.com/CAMeL-Lab/CamelProp
[2]Arabic HSB Romanization (Habash et al., 2007).

Proceedings of the 2nd Workshop on Advancing Natural Language Processing for Wikipedia (WikiNLP 2025), pages 31–44
August 1, 2025

morphology, and historical ad hoc conventions.

Diacritization, or diacritic restoration, aims at recovering omitted diacritics in languages that rely on them for disambiguation (Alqahtani et al., 2019; Darwish et al., 2017; Abandah et al., 2015). While both transliteration and diacritization have been well studied for Arabic, they are typically treated in isolation. An exception is the work of Mubarak et al. (2009), which considers both in the context of Arabic to English proper noun transliteration.

Lemmatization maps inflected words to their base forms. This is particularly important for morphologically rich languages such as Arabic (Roth et al., 2008). In the context of Wikipedia entries, providing the lemmas is useful to readers as it gives them a grounding on how to interpret and later inflect the word forms properly.

More concretely, we focus here on mapping pairs of undiacritized Arabic proper nouns and their English glosses to fully diacritized and lemmatized Arabic forms. The task can be viewed as partial transliteration, where Roman-script vowels help infer (or transliterate into) Arabic diacritical marks. For example, نخجوان *nxjwAn* 'Nakhchivan' (from Figure 1) should ideally be mapped to نَخْجِوَان *nax.jiwaAn*, rather than incorrect alternatives like نِخْجَوَان *nix.jawaAn* or نُخْجِوَان *nux.jiwaAn*.

We present a new dataset of 3,000 unique Arabic Wikipedia proper nouns annotated with gold lemma-level diacritizations. Each entry is paired with its English Wikipedia equivalent, enabling the study of joint diacritization and transliteration. We benchmark GPT-4o (OpenAI et al., 2024), which shows promising results but struggles with spelling variants and ambiguity. The dataset covers a range of named entities (people, places, and organizations) and includes 3,362 total pairs to reflect multiple valid diacritizations based on the gloss.

Our contributions are:

- A publicly available gold-standard dataset of Arabic Wikipedia proper nouns with English equivalents.[1]
- A GPT-4o benchmark and detailed error analysis for Arabic proper noun diacritization.

The remainder of this paper is structured as follows. Section 2 outlines Arabic linguistic aspects. Section 3 reviews related work. Sections 4 and 5 describe our dataset and annotation process. Section 6 presents evaluation results and error analysis.

Diacritic	Example		
Fatha	بَ	*ba*	/ba/
Damma	بُ	*bu*	/bu/
Kasra	بِ	*bi*	/bi/
Shadda	بّ	*b∼*	/bb/
Sukun	بْ	*b.*	/b/
Dagger Alif	بٰ	*bá*	/ba:/
Shadda + Fatha	بَّ	*b∼a*	/bba/
Shadda + Damma	بُّ	*b∼u*	/bbu/
Shadda + Kasra	بِّ	*b∼i*	/bbi/
Long vowel /a/	بَا	*baA*	/ba:/
Long vowel /u/	بُو	*buw*	/bu:/
Long vowel /i/	بِي	*biy*	/bi:/
Shadda + Long vowel /a/	بَّا	*bbaA*	/bba:/
Shadda + Long vowel /u/	بُّو	*bbuw*	/bbu:/
Shadda + Long vowel /i/	بِّي	*bbiy*	/bbi:/
Glide w	بَوْ	*baw.*	/baw/
Glide y	بَيْ	*bay.*	/bay/

Table 1: Examples of Arabic diacritics, their transliterations, and phonological values. We exclude nunation diacritics as they are not used in our lemmas.

2 Linguistic Background

2.1 Arabic Diacritization

Arabic orthography follows an *Abjad* system (Daniels, 2013), where letters encode consonants and diacritical marks represent short vowels, nunation (case endings), gemination, and vowel absence. Diacritic clusters are typically limited to a Shadda (◌ّ ∼) followed by a short vowel or nunation diacritic. Three letters, ا *A*, و *w*, and ي *y* (henceforth *AWY*), encode long vowels when preceded by a matching short vowel and not followed by any diacritic: ◌َا *aA* (/a:/), ◌ُو *uw* (/u:/), and ◌ِي *iy* (/i:/). These letters are often used with foreign name transliterations to mark the vowel quality independent of length, e.g., بين *byn* 'Ben' or 'Bean'. The letters و and ي also serve as glides (/w/ and /y/) when preceded by ◌َ *a* and followed by a sukun (◌ْ .). The letter ا *A* functions as a carrier for initial short vowels (*Alif Wasla*, ٱ *Ä*). Additionally, Arabic

Input Arabic		Gloss	Lemma Arabic		Transformation
الست	*Alst*	Al-Sit	سِتّ	*sit∼*	DET → ϕ
الواس	*AlwAs*	Elvas	إِلْوَاس	*Ăil.waAws*	Bare Alif → Alif Hamza
العجم	*Alςjm*	Al-Ajam	عَجَم	*ςajam*	DET → ϕ
الغظاة	*AlγĎAħ*	Al-Ghadhah	غَظَاة	*γaĎaAħ*	DET → ϕ
فنزويليون	*fnzwylywn*	Venezuelans	فِنِزْوِيلِيّ	*finiz.wiyliy∼*	3MP → ϕ
الجيبوتيون	*Aljybwtywn*	Djiboutians	جِيبُوتِيّ	*jiybuwtiy∼*	DET+3MP → ϕ

Table 2: Examples of lemmatization transformations from Arabic input (inflected) words to canonical lemmas, with English glosses and corresponding changes.

uses letters with attached Hamza diacritics, e.g., أ *Â*, إ *Ǎ*, آ *Ā*, ؤ *ŵ*, and ئ *ŷ*. The omission of Hamzas is treated as a spelling error and corrected during diacritization.

See Table 1 for examples, and Darwish et al. (2017) and Elgamal et al. (2024) for more details on Arabic diacritics.

2.2 Arabic Lemmatization

In Arabic morphology, the lemma is the canonical form (also known as citation form) of a word that abstracts over its inflected variants, including gender, number, person, and case, as well as attached clitics (Roth et al., 2008; Habash, 2010). Table 2 shows examples of input forms and their corresponding lemmas. In our context, lemmatization is simpler than in free-form text: we focus only on proper nouns, an English gloss is available to guide vowelization, and clitics are rare. The main challenges are distinguishing between base-word and determiner uses of ال *Al* (DET) initial substring (see Table 2 rows 1-2), and handling plural endings (3MP) ون *uw* in demonyms (Table 2 rows 5-6).

2.3 Arabic Transliterations

Transliteration from Roman script to Arabic script presents several challenges, primarily due to the misalignment between the phonology of the original language and its Roman script orthography, as well as differences between the phonology of the original languages and Arabic. Arabic, for example, has fewer vowels (6 in Arabic vs. 15 in English), and some missing (no /p/ or /v/) and additional consonants (e.g., emphatic /d/ and /q/). Arabic dialects vary in phonology, including sound quality, letter mapping, and syllabification, leading to multiple valid transliterations. For instance, the borrowed word 'plastic' can have different pronunciations and spellings, reflecting variations in vowels and syllabification (see Table 3). During annotation, we followed Wikipedia spelling and aligned with the English gloss. The team included Egyptian, Sudanese, and Levantine speakers, with an Egyptian speaker as the primary annotator.

	Pronunciation	Arabic	Transliteration
(a)	/bla:stik/	بْلَاسْتِك	*b.laAs.tik*
(b)	/bila:stik/	بِلَاسْتِك	*bilaAstik*
(c)	/bla:stik/	بْلَاسْتِيك	*b.laAs.tiyk*
(d)	/bila:stik/	بِلَاسْتِيك	*bilaAstiyk*
(e)	/bla:sti:k/	بْلَاسْتِيك	*b.laAs.tiyk*
(f)	/bila:sti:k/	بِلَاسْتِيك	*bilaAstiyk*
(g)	/bala:sti:k/	بَلَاسْتِيك	*balaAstiyk*
(h)	/ibla:stik/	إِبْلَاسْتِيك	*Aib.laAs.tiyk*

Table 3: Variants of the pronunciation and transliteration of the Arabic word for 'plastic'. Three basic spellings: (a-b) بلاستك *blAstk*, (c-g) بلاستيك *blAstyk*, and (h) ابلاستك *AblAstk*, with various diacritizations.

3 Related Work

3.1 Diacritization in Arabic NLP

Arabic diacritization has been extensively studied using both statistical and neural methods. Some approaches treat it as a standalone task (Zitouni et al., 2006; Mubarak et al., 2019), while others integrate it into multitask learning frameworks alongside linguistically related tasks such as part-of-speech tagging (Habash and Rambow, 2005; Alqahtani et al., 2020).

A commonly adopted strategy involves the use of morphological analyzers. For instance, Camelira (Camel Tools) implements an analyze-and-disambiguate pipeline: a morphological analyzer generates candidate analyses, which are then ranked by a classifier (Obeid et al., 2020, 2022). Similarly, Farasa uses morphological patterns to diacritize words (Darwish et al., 2017).

Systems such as Farasa and Camel Tools have demonstrated strong performance on sentence-level diacritization tasks. However, these systems are not directly applicable to our task, which centers on isolated proper nouns, adheres to a task-specific diacritization schema, and incorporates lemma mapping. Unlike sentence-based systems that leverage surrounding context for disambiguation, our task involves context-free diacritization, which poses distinct challenges (see Section 5.1).

3.2 Lemmatization in Arabic NLP

Lemmatization is another core task in Arabic NLP, and several tools offer robust performance across a variety of syntactic categories (Obeid et al., 2020, 2022; Jarrar et al., 2024). However, our lemmatization task has a narrower scope: it is limited to proper nouns that have a limited inflectional space (see Section 5.1 for further details on our lemmatization space).

3.3 Transliteration in Arabic NLP

Earlier research on Arabic–English transliteration relied on statistical approaches (Abduljaleel and Larkey, 2004), followed by more targeted work on proper nouns using models such as phonemic memory networks (Tian et al., 2022). A persistent challenge in this area is the lack of standardization in transliterating foreign names into Arabic, a problem exacerbated by the omission of diacritics (Aziz, 1983; Odisho, 1992).

To address the lack of standardization and limited resources, we introduce a new dataset and annotation guidelines specifically designed for the task of utilizing proper noun transliteration as a signal for Arabic diacritization.

Prior efforts investigated the intersection of transliteration and diacritization, such as Mubarak et al. (2009) and Darwish et al. (2017). Mubarak et al. (2009) used diacritization as a preprocessing step to transliteration. Although, the approach presented in Darwish et al. (2017) for automatically diacritizing transliterated words included leveraging English transliterations to generate Arabic diacritized proper nouns, both their training and test sets were limited in size (500 and 200 instances, respectively). Our resource, in contrast, is publicly available, much larger (3,000 diacritized lemmas), and benchmarked for robust evaluation and development.

3.4 Arabic Proper Noun Resources

Although various Arabic proper noun datasets exist, they often suffer from limited accessibility, lack of diacritics, or domain constraints. For example, Matthews (2007) compiled a list of 10,001 Arabic names, but the dataset is not publicly available. Eryani and Habash (2021) provide automatically Romanized Arabic bibliographic entries without diacritics, and both the Dan database (Halpern et al., 2009) and SAMA Graff et al. (2009) include diacritized proper nouns, but they were mainly collected form news sources.

Khairallah et al. (2024) released a large set of proper nouns as part of their CamelMorph Arabic morphological analyzer (henceforth CAMELPROP, CP for short). The dataset consists of two distinct portions: (a) CP-SAMA, which extends the SAMA (Graff et al., 2009) proper-noun list and updates their diacritizations; and (b) CP-WIKI which comprises 63K entries extracted from a Wikidata dump (14-Mar-2023).[3] The CP-WIKI was filtered by Khairallah et al. (2024) to include only single word entities in Arabic and English, and covering only personal and family names, locations and organizations. Unfortunately, Khairallah et al. (2024) did not provide diacritizations for the CP-WIKI portion. Our interest in this topic started by this problem in their open-source resource, which was not usable for our purposes. We discuss these datasets further in Section 4.

In this work, we present the first publicly available dataset of maximally manually diacritized and lemmatized Arabic proper nouns on a portion of the CP-WIKI dataset sourced from Wikimedia and manually annotated using English equivalents in a consistent and standardized annotation scheme. To support future work, we also release detailed annotation guidelines and provide the first benchmark of GPT-4o's performance on this task, offering a new resource for evaluating Arabic proper noun diacritization and transliteration.

[3] `https://dumps.wikimedia.org/wikidatawiki/entities/`

	CP-SAMA	CP-WIKI	CP-WIKI-D3K
Unique Arabic	6,022	63,417	3,000
Arabic-English Entries	7,202	71,251	3,362
English glosses per entry	1.20	1.12	1.12
Average Freq	205,077	97,438	61,544
Median Freq	11,732	87	75
Average Freeman Score	0.92	0.91	0.91
Diacritizations	Yes	No	Yes

Table 4: Comparison of dataset statistics across CP-SAMA, CP-WIKI, and the annotated subset CP-WIKI-D3K.

Class	CP-WIKI	CP-WIKI-D3K
Location	77.1%	85.2%
Name	25.5%	35.0%
Organization	2.0%	2.0%

Table 5: Distribution of different named entity classes across CP-WIKI and CP-WIKI-D3K

4 Datasets

We work with the CAMELPROP dataset, released as part of CamelMorph, an Arabic morphological analyzer, by Khairallah et al. (2024). As noted in Section 3, it consists of two parts: CP-SAMA and CP-WIKI. We randomly selected 3,000 unique Arabic-script proper nouns from CP-WIKI for manual annotation, forming our dataset CP-WIKI-D3K.

Table 4 compares the three datasets in terms of unique Arabic entries and full Arabic–English gloss pairs, average and median frequency and Arabic-English phonological similarity. For frequency we used the Arabic Frequency list from Khalifa et al. (2021). For phonological similarity, we used the Freeman similarity score (Freeman et al., 2006). The original data included multiple glosses per Arabic word (12–20% extra on average). We normalized this by splitting them into separate one-to-one pairs. For example, آنا *ĀnA*, glossed as 'A'ana; Ana; Anna', became three distinct entries: (آنا *ĀnA*, 'A'ana'), (آنا *ĀnA*, 'Ana'), and (آنا *ĀnA*, 'Anna'). Thus, our 3,000 Arabic words expanded to 3,362 Arabic–gloss pairs. While phonological similarity is only slightly lower in CP-WIKI-D3K and CP-WIKI, the overall frequency in CP-WIKI and CP-WIKI-D3K is significantly lower than CP-SAMA, highlighting the importance of modeling the diacritization of low-frequency proper nouns in Wikipedia and NLP.

In addition to frequency and phonological similarity, we examined the distribution of named entity categories, namely, personal and family names, locations, and organizations, across both the original CP-WIKI dataset and the manually annotated subset, CP-WIKI-D3K. The distributions were broadly similar, with location entities being the majority in both (CP-WIKI: 77.1%, CP-WIKI-D3K: 85.2%), followed by names and organizations. This consistency supports the representativeness of CP-WIKI-D3K for studying diacritization across entity types. Table 5 reports the detailed percentage breakdown of entity classes in both datasets.

5 Data Annotation

In this section, we discuss the diacritization guidelines we used, as well as the setup for initial automatic processing followed by manual correction.

5.1 Diacritization Guidelines

We follow the Arabic maximal diacritization guidelines as presented in Elgamal et al. (2024) with a small number of modifications to fit the purpose of our task. We list the most important decisions that are different from standard Arabic diacritization.

The Lemmatization Requirement This effort focuses exclusively on the diacritization of proper nouns and mapping them to their lemmas. As such, we require the removal of clitics such as the definite article and the removal of plural suffixes (see Section 2.2).

Input Spelling Integrity Aside from the minimal changes connected to lemmatization, and cor-

Invalid Lemma		Gloss	Issue	Corrected Lemma	
سانشِيز	*sAnšiyz*	Sanchez	Long vowels require preceding diacritics	سَانْشِيز	*saAn.šiyz*
كَرَمُ	*karamu*	Karam	Final letter cannot have a diacritic	كَرَم	*karam*
عَضُّوم	*ςaDu∼wm*	Addoum	Short diacritic cannot precede Shadda	عَضُّوم	*ςaD∼uwm*

Table 6: Examples of malformed words and their corrected lemmas with transliterations.

rections of the obligatory Hamza diacritic in Alif Hamza forms (see Section 2.1), we do not add, remove, or modify any letters in the provided input.

Consonant Clusters in Foreign Names While standard Arabic generally avoids consonant clusters, our dataset includes many foreign proper nouns where such clusters are phonetically natural. To more faithfully capture their pronunciation, we allowed forms with consecutive consonants, either multiple letters marked with Sukuns, or a Sukun followed by a letter with Shadda (geminated), even though this departs from Standard Arabic diacritization norms. For example, إلكتريك *Ălktryk* 'Electric' should be diacritized as إِلِكْتْرِيك *Ăilik.t.riyk* (with the consonant cluster /tr/), and زدينيك *zdynyk* 'Zdeněk' should be diacrtized as زْدِنِيك *z.diniyk* with initial /zd/ cluster.

Final Letter Ya The final letter ي *y* has multiple diacritizations that overlap with changes in dialectal Arabic, i.e. the softening of final y-gemination into /i/. As such, we had to dedicate part of the guidelines to outline the rules for diacritizing it as a geminated /yy/, a long vowel /i:/ or a glide /ay/.

The geminated version is the most specific in requirements with three possible cases:

- The gemination comes from the root or pattern of the word such as the final Ya in رَخِيّ *raxiy∼* 'Ar-Rakhi'.
- The lemma can be interpreted as having the derivational attribution suffix Ya-Nisba, e.g., إِشْبِيلِيّ *Ăiš.biyliy∼* 'Sevillian' (of or related to إِشْبِيلِيَّة *Ăiš.biyliy∼aħ* 'Seville').
- Gemination is necessary to reflect the pronunciation of certain foreign names, such as أَرْكْوِيّ *Âar.k.wiy∼* 'Arcueil'.

For other cases, if the final vowel sounds like a short /i/ or a long /i:/ and has a corresponding ي *y*, it is diacritized resembling a long vowel, e.g., أغاسي *ÂgAsy* Agassi, should be diacritized as أَغَاسِي *ÂagaAsiy*. The glide version is straightforward as it has a distinct phonological signal. One example is the word نَي *nay* 'Ney'.

Checking Well-formedness To ensure consistency with our annotation guidelines, we implemented automated checks to validate the well-formedness of diacritized lemmas. While these checks do not guarantee correctness, they are effective at identifying common errors and inconsistencies. We use these checks on both human and automatic annotations. See Table 6 for examples.

5.2 Initial Automatic Diacritization

To speed up the annotation process, we gave our annotator an automatically diacirtized version of the data. We used GPT-4o with Arabic Input and English Gloss (comparable to the best setting in Section 6). At the time of generating the initial automatic diacritization, we considered this a reasonable starting point.

GPT-4o postprocessing The output of GPT-4o was not always usable as is. When applying well-formedness checks to the diacritized outputs generated by GPT-4o, we observed several recurring patterns of errors that compromised the validity of the diacritized forms. In response, we developed an automated pipeline specifically aimed at correcting these systematic errors.[1] The automatic correction procedures included the following operations:

- Insertion of Fatha before Alif (ا *A*).
- Insertion of Kasra after Alif-Hamza-Below (إ *Ă*).
- Normalization of Shadda-Vowel clusters such that the vowel diacritic follows the Shadda diacritic.
- Removal of final diacritics as lemmas do not have them.

Type of Disagreement	Freq	Gloss	First Annotator	Second Annotator
Kasra ↔ Sukun	13	Tibet	تِبِت tibit	تِبْت tib.t
Kasra ↔ Fatha	9	Shechem	شِكِيم šikiym	شَكِيم šakiym
Consonant ↔ Long vowel	9	Jane	جَيْن jay.n	جِين jiyn
Sukun ↔ Damma	5	Acquaviva	أَكُوَافِيفَا ÂakuwaAfiyfaA	أَكْوَافِيفَا Âak.waAfiyfaA
Sukun ↔ Fatha	1	Aminadav	عَمِينْدَاف ςamiyn.daAf	عَمِينَدَاف ςamiynadaAf
Shadda ↔ ϕ	1	Oss	أُوسّ Âuws∼	أُوس Âuws

Table 7: Types of disagreements in Inter-Annotator Evaluation

- Insertion of missing Sukuns to indicate vowel absence at the end of syllable or in a consonant cluster.
- Removal of Fatha after Alif Madda (آ $\bar{A}$).
- Mapping Non-Arabic Arabic-script letters, such as those used in Urdu or Persian, to their closest Arabic language form.

5.3 Manual Diacritization

The manual diacritization and quality checks were carried out by a native speaker of Arabic from Egypt who is a trained linguist and a highly experienced annotator. The annotation process initially was done in tandem with the finalization of the guidelines with a team of the authors working jointly to optimize the quality of the annotation. The annotator was provided an Arabic word, along with its English gloss, and a proposed diacritization from GPT-4o after being refined by the automatic post-process described above. The annotations were carried on Google Sheets in a very simple setup. The annotator reviewed the proposed diacritization making changes where needed in accordance to the guidelines. The annotator made changes to 909 proposed lemmas out of 3,362 (∼27%). In 213 instances (6.3% of all entries), there was a change connected with lemmatization: 74% relative involved the Al determiner, 22.5% a change in Alif-Hamza spelling, and 3.3% involving the demonym plural ending.

5.4 Inter-annotator Agreement

To assess the quality of our annotation and the consistency of our guidelines, we conducted an inter-annotator agreement study. A second annotator, a native Arabic speaker from Egypt, independently re-annotated a subset of 500 randomly selected samples from the dataset, utilizing the same annotation process and adhering to the same guidelines as the first annotator. Out of the 500 samples, the annotators fully agreed on 462 instances and disagreed on 38, resulting in an inter-annotator agreement rate of 92.4%. Table 7 presents the various types of inter-annotator disagreements along with their corresponding frequencies. Each row in the table represents a type of disagreement where the annotators selected different diacritics for the same word. For example, the first row shows instances where either one of the annotators chose a Kasra while the other selected a Sukun.

6 Evaluation

6.1 Experimental Setup

We perform computational experiments to perform the task of diacritization of proper nouns. For this, we prompt GPT-4o on all of the annotated dataset described in Section 5. We prompt the model with different input formats to assess its capabilities while giving it different levels of information: the inputs and the number of examples shown to the model (shots). We used default settings for optional parameters (e.g., temperature, top_p) from the gpt-4o-2024-11-20 snapshot.[4]

Inputs The model is given a detailed description of the task to be performed. Our main experiments reflect all the information given to our annotator, where we provide the model with both the Arabic Input and the English Gloss (**Arabic + Gloss**). Additionally, we also experiment with a more constrained setup where the model is provided solely with the the Arabic Input (**Arabic Only**).

[4]https://platform.openai.com/docs/api-reference/chat/create

Input Format	Shots	Accuracy	Distance
Arabic + Gloss	Zero	46.5%	1.02
Arabic + Gloss	One	61.9%	0.64
Arabic + Gloss	Few	**73.0%**	0.41
Arabic Only	Zero	36.7%	1.29
Arabic Only	One	49.7%	0.86
Arabic Only	Few	55.9%	0.71

Table 8: GPT-4o model results on CP-WIKI-D3K in terms of exact match accuracy and Levenshtein edit distance.

Shots In addition to the different inputs, we also consider further experiments where we supply the model with varying number of examples to learn from[1] Hence, in addition to just providing the input to diacritize (**Zero-Shot**), we also supply the model with a single example (**One-Shot**), and 80 examples (**Few-Shot**). The examples are randomly sampled from the CP-SAMA data. The one-shot and few-shot examples were selected once and reused across all model prompts. However, since CP-SAMA has fully lemmatized Arabic Inputs, we manually manipulated some of the examples to have a representation of clitic removal and Hamza normalization. Refer to Appendix A for a more detailed description of the prompts used.

Post-processing As a post-processing step, the outputs were ran through the same processing pipeline mentioned in Section 5.2. To evaluate the performance of the different experiments, we computed two metrics: accuracy by measuring the exact match between the post-processed output and the gold-standard diacritization and Levenshtein edit distance (Levenshtein, 1966) between the output and gold-standard diacritization.

6.2 Results

The results demonstrate that while diacritizing proper nouns remains a challenging task, incorporating the English gloss offers a valuable signal for the model. Notably, the best performance is achieved with few-shot, showing the effectiveness of providing a diverse and representative sample. Table 8 shows the results with different prompts.

6.3 Interplay of Frequency, Similarity, and Accuracy

We investigated how lexical frequency and phonological similarity (Freeman et al., 2006) affect model performance under our best configuration: few-shot prompting with Arabic + Gloss.

The Freeman similarity score averaged a high 91% across the dataset, consistent with the transliteration focus of the task. We binned the data into 10 intervals based on Freeman score. The lowest-similarity bins (up to 50%), comprising only 3% of the data, contained mostly high-frequency named entities and translations, e.g., مصر *mSr* for 'Egypt' and عمالاق *ςmlAq* for 'jötnar'. Despite their low similarity, this group achieved 13.9% higher accuracy and had, on average, 10 times the frequency compared to the rest of the data. The bins up to 90% similarity comprised 35% of the data; their average frequency is only 5% higher than the last bin, but their average accuracy is lower by 3.6% absolute.

We found strong negative correlation between accuracy and edit distance (-0.95), confirming that higher accuracy aligns with fewer character edits. Frequency and Freeman score showed a moderate negative correlation (-0.69), likely due to high-frequency translated names. Freeman similarity and accuracy were also moderately negatively correlated (-0.70), indicating that frequent but phonetically dissimilar words are still predicted accurately.

We analyzed performance across frequency quartiles (Q1 to Q4). Accuracy rose steadily from 65% in Q1 to 80% in Q4. The correlation between average frequency and accuracy across quartiles was 0.68, confirming the positive impact of frequency on model performance. Full analysis tables are presented in Appendix B.

6.4 Error Analysis

We analyzed errors from a randomly selected sample of 1,010 output entries from the best performing setup from Section 6.2, and classified errors into several categories based on observed patterns. There were 740 (73.3%) exact matches (correct generations).

Of the 270 (26.7%) errors, there were 175 cases where the error was only diacritization differences. See examples in Table 9. Upon further analysis of this class of errors, we found that the model overpredicts Fathas (+25%) and Shaddas (+96%), while underpredicting Kasras (-18%) and Sukuns (-23%), indicating imbalanced vowel modeling and overuse of gemination.

The next largest class of errors, 60 cases, were those with spelling changes limited to the set of

Input	Gloss	Reference	Prediction	Error Type
العمود Alςmwd	Al-Amud	عَمُود ςamuwd	عَمُود ςamuwd	Exact Match
أفراموفو ÂfrAmwfw	Avramovo	أَفْرَامُوفُو Âaf.raAmuwfuw	أَفْرَامُوفُو Âaf.raAmuwfuw	Exact Match
هاغن hAγn	Hagen	هَاغِن haAγin	هَاغِن haAγin	Exact Match
إشتهارد ĂšthArd	Eshtehard	إِشْتِهَارْد Ăiš.tihaAr.d	إِشْتَهَارْد Ăiš.tahaAr.d	Diac
بلاجيفيتش blAjyfytš	Blažević	بْلَاجِيفِيتْش b.laAjiyfiyt.š	بِلَاجِيفِيتْش bilaAjiyfiyt.š	Diac
دسوق dswq	Desouk	دِسُوق disuwq	دُسُوق dusuwq	Diac
ريبلاي ryblAy	Ripley	رِيبْلَاي riyb.laAy	رِيبْلِي riyb.liy	*AWY*
ريكسينغين ryksynγyn	Rexingen	رِيكْسِينْغِين riyk.siyn.γiyn	رِيكْسِنْغِن riyk.sin.γin	*AWY*
جوندريزيك jwndryzyk	Gondrezick	جُونْدْرِيزِيك juwn.d.riyziyk	جُنْدْرِيزِيك jun.d.riyziyk	*AWY*
ميشيغان myšyγAn	Michigan	مِيشِيغَان miyšiyγaAn	مِيشِيجَان miyšiyjaAn	$j \leftrightarrow \gamma$
تسيخانوف tsyxAnwf	Ciechanów	تِسِيخَانُوف tisiyxaAnuwf	تِسِيهَانُوف tisiyhaAnuwf	$h \leftrightarrow x$
أردينة Ârdynħ	Ardineh	أَرْدِينَة Âar.diynaħ	أَرْدِينَه Âar.diynah	$\hbar \leftrightarrow h$
إيغيل Ăyγyl	Eagle	إِيغِيل Ăiyγiyl	إِيجِل Ăiyjil	Multiple
كرامة krAmħ	Gourrama	كُرَامَة kuraAmaħ	كُورَامَا kuwraAmaA	Multiple
ايكوميديا AykwmydyA	Eco-Médias	إِيكُومِيدْيَا Ăiykuwmiyd.yaA	إِيكُومِيدْيَآس Ăiykuwmiyd.yaĀs	Multiple
بارافرانكا bArAfrAnkA	Barrafranca	بَارّ افْرَانْكَا baAr aAf.raAn.kaA	بَارَافْرَانْكَة baAraAf.raAn.kaħ	Multiple

Table 9: Examples of evaluated instances along with their, reference and predicted diacritized forms, and corresponding error types. The error categories are diacritic mismatches (Diac), *AWY* spelling changes (*AWY*), several consonant and ta-marbuta substitutions ($j \leftrightarrow \gamma$, $h \leftrightarrow x$, and $\hbar \leftrightarrow h$), and those with multiple changes (Multiple).

long vowel (and glides) letters ا *A*, و *w*, and ي *y* (*AWY*). As we see in the examples in Table 9, the model has the tendency of dropping such letters rather than adding them. Another class of errors, 10 cases, are those with specific letter replacements such as ج $j \leftrightarrow$ غ γ, خ $x \leftrightarrow$ ه h, and ة $\hbar \leftrightarrow$ ه h. The final class of errors, 25 cases, are those with multiple changes happening at once.

While these cases don't match the gold reference, they are plausible and acceptable alternatives in most cases, especially in the context of linguistic variation discussed in Section 2. For example, the generated diacritization for بلاجيفيتش *blAjyfytš* 'Blažević' as seen in Table 9 (row 5), follows the common phenomena of breaking word initial complex onsets in many spoken dialects of Arabic and in MSA. Another example is the entry ايكوميديا *AykwmydyA* 'Eco-Médias', where the input follows a pronunciation-based transliteration while the generated form adhered to the orthography of the gloss.

These variations highlight the need for modeling techniques and evaluation metrics that account for this aspect of Arabic proper noun diacritization, which in turn requires additional annotated data.

7 Conclusion and Future Work

We presented a new 3,362 entry dataset of Arabic Wikipedia proper nouns annotated with gold-standard lemma diacritizations, paired with their English equivalents. This resource enables the joint study of diacritization and transliteration in a realistic setting characterized by ambiguity and spelling variation. We benchmarked GPT-4o on this task, providing insights into its capabilities and limitations. While the model performs reasonably well, especially on frequent names, it struggles with rarer entries and variant mappings.

Looking ahead, we plan to expand the dataset with more diverse names, integrate it into a morphological analyzer, and explore fine-tuned models for diacritizing proper nouns in broader contexts. We also plan to fine-tune dedicated models for this task and develop more robust approaches to name ambiguity, especially with multiple valid diacritizations. We hope this resource advances Arabic NLP and name normalization in multilingual settings like Wikipedia.

Limitations

A primary limitation of this work lies in the inherent subjectivity of diacritization, particularly for proper nouns where multiple correct variants may exist depending on regional, historical, or phonetic conventions. Despite rigorous annotation guidelines and quality checks, variability is an inevitable aspect of any human-annotated linguistic resource. Our current benchmark relies solely on GPT-4o, and we acknowledge the importance of evaluating performance across a broader range of large language models. While initial results are promising, the overall performance remains limited and, in our assessment, not yet suitable for reliable downstream use.

Ethics Statement

All data used in this project were sourced from publicly available Arabic Wikipedia entries and their corresponding English titles, in accordance with Wikimedia's terms of use. The annotation process was conducted transparently and ethically, with fair compensation provided to the annotators. We make both the corpus and the annotation guidelines publicly accessible under an open license, supporting reproducibility and community collaboration. Our goal is to contribute a valuable resource for Arabic language processing and to aid the broader Wikimedia effort by enhancing the quality of Arabic Wikipedia entries. Finally, we acknowledge that all NLP tools and resources can be used with malicious intent; this is not our intention, and we categorically discourage it.

Benefits

This work directly supports the Wikimedia community by enhancing the quality and accessibility of Arabic Wikipedia content. By providing more accurate diacritization for proper nouns from all over the world on Arabic Wikipedia, we aim to improve readability, pronunciation, and downstream tasks such as named entity recognition and machine translation. The dataset, code, and annotation guidelines are all released under the Creative Commons Attribution-ShareAlike (CC BY-SA) license to ensure community reuse and adaptation. Filtering was applied to select single-word proper nouns related to people, locations, and organizations, drawn from Arabic Wikipedia entries that have clear English counterparts, thereby supporting multilingual alignment and cross-lingual research.

Risks

Our project poses no known risks to Wikimedia editors or contributors. We do not name, identify, or reference any individual editor (by username or otherwise), nor do we expose any metadata that could be used to infer editor identities. The work focuses solely on content-level linguistic annotation and transformation. There are no known ways in which this research could be used to derive sensitive or personal information about contributors, and we strongly discourage any attempts to repurpose the resource for such purposes.

Acknowledgments

We would like to express our sincere gratitude to Hamdy Mubarak for his valuable insights and his generous willingness to answer our questions throughout the course of this work. We thank Djellel Difallah for advice on initial data collection. We would like to also thank Bashar Alhafni and Mostafa Saeed for their insightful discussions and helpful conversations.

References

Gheith A. Abandah, Alex Graves, Balkees Al-Shagoor, Alaa Arabiyat, Fuad Jamour, and Majid Al-Taee. 2015. Automatic diacritization of Arabic text using recurrent neural networks. *International Journal on Document Analysis and Recognition (IJDAR)*, 18(2):183–197.

Nasreen Abduljaleel and Leah Larkey. 2004. English to Arabic transliteration for information retrieval: A statistical approach.

Sawsan Alqahtani, Ajay Mishra, and Mona Diab. 2019. Efficient convolutional neural networks for diacritic restoration. In *Proceedings of the 2019 Conference on Empirical Methods in Natural Language Processing and the 9th International Joint Conference on Natural Language Processing (EMNLP-IJCNLP)*, pages 1442–1448, Hong Kong, China. Association for Computational Linguistics.

Sawsan Alqahtani, Ajay Mishra, and Mona Diab. 2020. A multitask learning approach for diacritic restoration. In *Proceedings of the 58th Annual Meeting of the Association for Computational Linguistics*, pages 8238–8247, Online. Association for Computational Linguistics.

Yowell Aziz. 1983. Transliteration of English proper nouns into Arabic. *Meta*, 28(1):70–84.

Kenneth R. Beesley. 1997. Romanization, Transcription and Transliteration. Http://www.xrce.xerox.com/Research-Development/Historical-projects/Linguistic-Demos/Arabic-Morphological-Analysis-and-

Generation/Romanization-Transcription-and-Transliteration.

Fernando Benites, Gilbert François Duivesteijn, Pius von Däniken, and Mark Cieliebak. 2020. TRANSLIT: A large-scale name transliteration resource. In *Proceedings of the Twelfth Language Resources and Evaluation Conference*, pages 3265–3271, Marseille, France. European Language Resources Association.

Nancy Chen, Rafael E. Banchs, Min Zhang, Xiangyu Duan, and Haizhou Li. 2018. Report of NEWS 2018 named entity transliteration shared task. In *Proceedings of the Seventh Named Entities Workshop*, pages 55–73, Melbourne, Australia. Association for Computational Linguistics.

Peter T Daniels. 2013. The Arabic writing system. *The Oxford handbook of Arabic linguistics*, pages 422–431.

Kareem Darwish, Hamdy Mubarak, and Ahmed Abdelali. 2017. Arabic diacritization: Stats, rules, and hacks. In *Proceedings of the Third Arabic Natural Language Processing Workshop*, pages 9–17, Valencia, Spain. Association for Computational Linguistics.

Salman Elgamal, Ossama Obeid, Mhd Kabbani, Go Inoue, and Nizar Habash. 2024. Arabic diacritics in the wild: Exploiting opportunities for improved diacritization. In *Proceedings of the 62nd Annual Meeting of the Association for Computational Linguistics (Volume 1: Long Papers)*, pages 14815–14829, Bangkok, Thailand. Association for Computational Linguistics.

Fadhl Eryani and Nizar Habash. 2021. Automatic Romanization of Arabic bibliographic records. In *Proceedings of the Sixth Arabic Natural Language Processing Workshop*, pages 213–218, Kyiv, Ukraine (Virtual). Association for Computational Linguistics.

Andrew Freeman, Sherri Condon, and Christopher Ackerman. 2006. Cross linguistic name matching in English and Arabic. In *Proceedings of the Conference of the North American Chapter of the Association for Computational Linguistics (NAACL)*, pages 471–478, New York City, NY.

David Graff, Mohamed Maamouri, Basma Bouziri, Sondos Krouna, Seth Kulick, and Tim Buckwalter. 2009. Standard Arabic Morphological Analyzer (SAMA) Version 3.1. Linguistic Data Consortium LDC2009E73.

Nizar Habash and Owen Rambow. 2005. Arabic tokenization, part-of-speech tagging and morphological disambiguation in one fell swoop. In *Proceedings of the 43rd Annual Meeting of the Association for Computational Linguistics (ACL'05)*, pages 573–580, Ann Arbor, Michigan. Association for Computational Linguistics.

Nizar Habash, Abdelhadi Soudi, and Tim Buckwalter. 2007. On Arabic Transliteration. In A. van den Bosch and A. Soudi, editors, *Arabic Computational Morphology: Knowledge-based and Empirical Methods*, pages 15–22. Springer, Netherlands.

Nizar Y Habash. 2010. *Introduction to Arabic natural language processing*, volume 3. Morgan & Claypool Publishers.

Jack Halpern et al. 2009. Lexicon-driven approach to the recognition of Arabic named entities. In *Proceedings of the Second International Conference on Arabic Language Resources and Tools*, pages 193–198. Citeseer.

Mustafa Jarrar, Diyam Akra, and Tymaa Hammouda. 2024. Alma: Fast lemmatizer and pos tagger for Arabic. *Procedia Computer Science*, 244:378–387. 6th International Conference on AI in Computational Linguistics.

Christian Khairallah, Salam Khalifa, Reham Marzouk, Mayar Nassar, and Nizar Habash. 2024. Camel morph MSA: A large-scale open-source morphological analyzer for Modern Standard Arabic. In *Proceedings of the 2024 Joint International Conference on Computational Linguistics, Language Resources and Evaluation (LREC-COLING 2024)*, pages 2683–2691, Torino, Italia. ELRA and ICCL.

Salam Khalifa, Go Inoue, Bashar Alhafni, Nurpeiis Baimukan, Houda Bouamor, and Nizar Habash. 2021. Camel Arabic Frequency Lists .

V. I. Levenshtein. 1966. Binary Codes Capable of Correcting Deletions, Insertions and Reversals. *Soviet Physics Doklady*, 10:707.

David Matthews. 2007. Transliteration using statistical machine translation. Master's thesis, University of Edinburgh, Edinburgh, United Kingdom. An automatic transliteration system built using Moses, modeled at the surface level with phrase-based SMT techniques.

Hamdy Mubarak, Ahmed Abdelali, Hassan Sajjad, Younes Samih, and Kareem Darwish. 2019. Highly effective Arabic diacritization using sequence to sequence modeling. In *Proceedings of the 2019 Conference of the North American Chapter of the Association for Computational Linguistics: Human Language Technologies, Volume 1 (Long and Short Papers)*, pages 2390–2395, Minneapolis, Minnesota. Association for Computational Linguistics.

Hamdy Mubarak, Mohamed Al Sharqawy, and Esraa Al Masry. 2009. Diacritization and transliteration of proper nouns from Arabic to English. In *Proceedings of the Second International Conference on Arabic Language Resources and Tools*, Cairo, Egypt. The MEDAR Consortium.

Ossama Obeid, Go Inoue, and Nizar Habash. 2022. Camelira: An Arabic multi-dialect morphological disambiguator. In *Proceedings of the 2022 Conference on Empirical Methods in Natural Language Processing: System Demonstrations*, pages 319–326, Abu Dhabi, UAE. Association for Computational Linguistics.

Ossama Obeid, Nasser Zalmout, Salam Khalifa, Dima Taji, Mai Oudah, Bashar Alhafni, Go Inoue, Fadhl Eryani, Alexander Erdmann, and Nizar Habash. 2020. CAMeL tools: An open source python toolkit for Arabic natural language processing. In *Proceedings of the Twelfth Language Resources and Evaluation Conference*, pages 7022–7032, Marseille, France. European Language Resources Association.

Edward Y. Odisho. 1992. Transliterating English in Arabic. *Zeitschrift für Arabische Linguistik*, 1(24):21–34.

OpenAI, Josh Achiam, Steven Adler, Sandhini Agarwal, Lama Ahmad, Ilge Akkaya, Florencia Leoni Aleman, Diogo Almeida, Janko Altenschmidt, Sam Altman, Shyamal Anadkat, Red Avila, Igor Babuschkin, et al. 2024. GPT-4 technical report. *Preprint*, arXiv:2303.08774.

Ryan Roth, Owen Rambow, Nizar Habash, Mona Diab, and Cynthia Rudin. 2008. Arabic morphological tagging, diacritization, and lemmatization using lexeme models and feature ranking. In *Proceedings of the Conference of the Association for Computational Linguistics (ACL)*, Columbus, Ohio.

Yuanhe Tian, Renze Lou, Xiangyu Pang, Lianxi Wang, Shengyi Jiang, and Yan Song. 2022. Improving English-Arabic transliteration with phonemic memories. In *Findings of the Association for Computational Linguistics: EMNLP 2022*, pages 3262–3272, Abu Dhabi, United Arab Emirates. Association for Computational Linguistics.

Imed Zitouni, Jeffrey S. Sorensen, and Ruhi Sarikaya. 2006. Maximum entropy based restoration of Arabic diacritics. In *Proceedings of the International Conference on Computational Linguistics and the Conference of the Association for Computational Linguistics (COLING-ACL)*, pages 577–584, Sydney, Australia.

A GPT-4o Prompts

In the system role, we provide the task description, and optionally, the few-shot demonstrations, when they are used. For the user role, we always provide the single instance to be diacritized. Table 10 lists all of the prompts used for the different settings. Table 11 shows a sample of the few-shot examples. These are formatted as a markdown table in the prompts.

Shots	Prompt
	Arabic Word+Gloss Input
Zero	You are an expert in Arabic. You are given the undiacritized proper noun in Arabic and its English gloss. Your task is to generate the corresponding diacritized proper noun lemma in Arabic. Arabic lemmas are dictionary entries that have no attached definite article (ال). Diacritization is adding the correct diacritic markings to undiacritized words. Remove the Arabic definite article (ال) when present. Do not add, remove, or substitute any other letters in the input. Determine the most accurate diacritization that matches the English gloss pronunciation. The user will provide a Markdown table with 1 rows. Each row contains an undiacritized proper noun in Arabic in the "Input" column and its English gloss in the "Gloss" column. Return exactly 1 diacritized lemmas, one per line. Do not include extra text, explanations, or formatting.
Few/One	You are an expert in Arabic. You are given the undiacritized proper noun in Arabic and its English gloss. Your task is to generate the corresponding diacritized proper noun lemma in Arabic. Arabic lemmas are dictionary entries that have no attached definite article (ال). Diacritization is adding the correct diacritic markings to undiacritized words. Remove the Arabic definite article (ال) when present. Do not add, remove, or substitute any other letters in the input. Determine the most accurate diacritization that matches the English gloss pronunciation. The user will provide a Markdown table with 1 rows. Each row contains an undiacritized proper noun in Arabic in the "Input" column and its English gloss in the "Gloss" column. Return exactly 1 diacritized lemmas, one per line. Do not include extra text, explanations, or formatting. Here are some examples of triplets of an undiacritized proper noun in Arabic ("Input"), its respective English gloss ("Gloss"), and its diacritized lemma ("Output") for reference `<Few-Shots-table>`
	Arabic Word Only Input
Zero	You are an expert in Arabic. You are given the undiacritized proper noun in Arabic. Your task is to generate the corresponding diacritized proper noun lemma in Arabic. Arabic lemmas are dictionary entries that have no attached definite article (ال). Diacritization is adding the correct diacritic markings to undiacritized words. Remove the Arabic definite article (ال) when present. Do not add, remove, or substitute any other letters in the input. The user will provide a Markdown table with 1 rows. Each row contains an undiacritized proper noun in Arabic in the "Input" column. Return exactly 1 diacritized lemmas, one per line. Do not include extra text, explanations, or formatting.
Few/One	You are an expert in Arabic. You are given the undiacritized proper noun in Arabic. Your task is to generate the corresponding diacritized proper noun lemma in Arabic. Arabic lemmas are dictionary entries that have no attached definite article (ال). Diacritization is adding the correct diacritic markings to undiacritized words. Remove the Arabic definite article (ال) when present. Do not add, remove, or substitute any other letters in the input. The user will provide a Markdown table with 1 rows. Each row contains an undiacritized proper noun in Arabic in the "Input" column. Return exactly 1 diacritized lemmas, one per line. Do not include extra text, explanations, or formatting. Here are some examples of pairs of an undiacritized proper noun in Arabic ("Input"), and its diacritized lemma ("Output") for reference `<Few-Shots-table>`

Table 10: System prompts used in the experiments. `<Few-Shots-table>` is a placeholder for few-shot examples. In either setting, the user prompts consist solely of a single instance to be diacritized.

Arabic Word		Gloss	Diacritized Reference	
ايدكس	*Aydks*	IDEX	إِيدِكس	*Ǎiydiks*
الغارديان	*AlgArdyAn*	Guardian	غَارْدِيَان	*gaAr.diyaAn*
رودريغيز	*rwdrygyz*	Rodriguez	رُودْرِيغِيز	*ruwd.riygiyz*
اوروغواي	*AwrwgwAy*	Uruguay	أُورُوغْوَاي	*Âuwruwg.waAy*
بوتيه	*bwtyh*	Boutier	بُوتِيِه	*buwtiyih*
وايزمن	*wAyzmn*	Weizman	وَايزْمَن	*waAyz.man*

Table 11: A sample of few-shot examples used for prompting GPT-4o

B Supplementary Interplay of Frequency, Similarity, and Accuracy

Freeman Bin	Instances	Instance %	Frequency	Matches	Accuracy	Distance
10%	6	0.2%	2,280,059	5	83.3%	0.17
20%	7	0.2%	454,346	6	85.7%	0.29
30%	23	0.7%	303,728	20	87.0%	0.22
40%	27	0.8%	690,729	23	85.2%	0.26
50%	26	0.8%	64,814	23	88.5%	0.12
60%	71	2.1%	30,274	45	63.4%	0.69
70%	164	4.9%	57,361	124	75.6%	0.37
80%	271	8.1%	22,803	185	68.3%	0.46
90%	587	17.5%	22,909	404	68.8%	0.52
100%	2,180	64.8%	60,343	1,619	74.3%	0.38
10–90%	1,182	35.2%	63,761	835	70.6%	0.48
10–50%	89	2.6%	496,420	77	86.5%	0.20
60–100%	3,273	97.4%	49,719	2,377	72.6%	0.42
All	3,362	100.0%	61,544	2,454	73.0%	0.41

Table 12: Accuracy, average frequency, and edit distance across Freeman similarity score bins.

Frequency Range	Instances	Average Freq.	Matches	Accuracy	Avg. Freeman
Q1 (lowest 25%)	787	2	510	64.8%	91.1%
Q2 (25–50%)	893	25	627	70.2%	90.4%
Q3 (50–75%)	840	567	646	76.9%	91.2%
Q4 (highest 25%)	842	245,145	671	79.7%	89.7%
All	3,362	61,544	2,454	72.99%	90.6%

Table 13: Accuracy, Average Frequency, and average Freeman similarity scores across word frequency quartiles.

Author Index

Association for Computational Linguistics
209 N. Eighth Street
Stroudsburg, Pennsylvania 18360

ISBN 979-8-3313-2421-6

CURRAN ASSOCIATES INC.
proceedings.com